Native
Women

CHANGING
THEIR WORLDS

Patricia J. Cutright

NATIVE VOICES
Summertown, TN

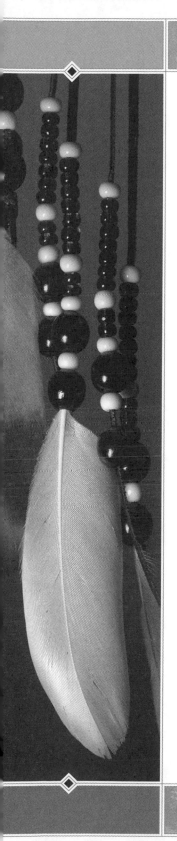

Library of Congress Cataloging-in-Publication Data available upon request

We chose to print this title on paper certified by The Forest Stewardship Council®
(FSC®), a global, not-for-profit organization dedicated to the promotion of responsible
forest management worldwide.

© 2021 Patricia J. Cutright
Cover and interior design: John Wincek

7th Generation
an imprint of BPC
PO Box 99
Summertown, TN 38483
888-260-8458
bookpubco.com
nativevoicesbooks.com

Printed in the United States of America

ISBN: 978-1-939053-32-9

Photo credits found on page 116.

26 25 24 23 22 21   2 3 4 5 6 7 8 9

For my husband, Ken, who has shared my story for more than three decades. He has been my sage, my best critic, and an indomitable, stalwart supporter. He brings light to my days and puts joy in my heart. *Philámayaye!* Thank you so very much!

CONTENTS

ACKNOWLEDGMENTS

ike many writers, my thoughts and words can come in herky-jerky fashion. Sometimes the script flows with no hesitation, but other times I am lost in rumination, stuck for the right word or just overwhelmed by the task at hand. The time and care given by many around me provided the motivation I needed to soldier on.

In memory of my father, Ernest Smith, who experienced such loss and pain in his life growing up on the rez but never denied us his love. To my siblings and their spouses—Kathy and Gary, Tommy and Linda, Randy and Ruth, and Terry— you have always believed in me. Throughout the years, your love and support have given me the confidence to overcome and charge ahead time and time again.

I owe so much to my mother and aunties, the Briggs sisters, whose lives are reflected in every page of this book. My sincere thanks to Cathy Bambrick, Joanna Thompson, archivist Troy Eller English, Della Nohl, and my editor, Kathie Hanson, for their ideas and assistance, good counsel, and unflagging enthusiasm. Heartfelt thanks would not be complete without acknowledging the love and support of Joan Downing, who I was lucky enough to have in my life for forty-eight years. And I am so grateful to those strong women in this book who took the time out of their busy lives to be interviewed. Thank you.

Indigenous women have historically been characterized in history books and literature as playing less dominant, even subservient, roles. In reality, Indigenous women have always been the strength behind their communities. They have been warriors, leaders, and change-makers who have valued the sanctity of family and worked to preserve the culture and language of their people. The stories told in this collection were researched and selected from more than one hundred amazing Native women. Some are well known, while others are just beginning to make their mark in this world. They all demonstrate the courage it takes to lean into challenges and succeed in education, politics, law, or any of the other careers they have chosen.

Where does my motivation come from to tell their stories? In the Native American tradition, the family circle is where we listen, observe, and learn through the oral tradition of "talk story." On the maternal side of my family, my aunties were some of the best at sharing the stories of their lives.

My mother and her eight sisters grew up on the wind-swept prairie of South Dakota on the Cheyenne River Reservation. In the 1920s and '30s, their sod-roofed house was nothing more than a one-room cabin with no indoor plumbing or electricity. Seven of the nine girls were the product of the US government's Indian boarding school system. The life they lived became hours of storytelling around the kitchen table. Oral history was shared with those of us who were lucky enough to sit quietly and absorb. Their stories described difficult times as well as good, but they always revealed an ability to overcome adversity and focus on the positive. It was in these stories that I forged my admiration for the strength and resilience found in Native women.

Like my mother and her sisters, the women in this book rose above the fray, believed in themselves, and changed the world around them. I am honored to share the stories of these remarkable Native American and First Nations women and hope their stories will reveal the potential we all have within ourselves.

Ashley Callingbull Burnham

ENOCH CREE NATION

You don't have to be condemned from day one just because you were born on a reserve.

ASHLEY CALLINGBULL BURNHAM

Imagine a little five-year-old girl, lying in a strange bed, surrounded by darkness, far from the comfortable home of her grandparents, fearful of the terror that happens in the night. All children have these fears, which are usually outgrown as the years go by. But for Ashley Callingbull, these fears were real, and they stayed with her into her teens, started by an unrelenting cycle of physical and sexual abuse committed by her mother's boyfriend. It was abuse that confused and destroyed Ashley's self-esteem, making her question her worth.

Ashley Callingbull Burnham is from the Enoch Cree Nation of Alberta, Canada, and was born on October 21, 1989. During the first five years of her life, she was raised in the traditional ways by her single mother, Lisa, and her maternal grandparents, Charlotte and George Callingbull. Her grandparents, a medicine man and woman, were considered healers in

Mrs. Universe 2015.

their community. They ran a sweat lodge in Enoch and lived their lives helping others in selfless ways. This caring was demonstrated by fostering more than twenty-six children that they brought into their home over the years. Ashley loved and respected her *kokum* ("grandmother" in the Cree language), who taught her the importance of her culture and to always be grateful for what she'd been given.

Ashley's world was turned upside down, though, when her mother moved the two of them to a town sixty miles from Enoch to join a man she was involved with at the time. Ashley started school there as her life was disintegrating around her. The man who promised to take care of the mother and her daughter was now their abuser. For six long years, Ashley and her mother lived in fear of physical and sexual assault. Lisa tried to provide for her family. She worked for the Cree Nation in Enoch, and that demanded traveling an hour to and from the job, leaving Ashley in the care of the boyfriend for long hours throughout the day. Although Ashley's mother was working hard, they lived in extreme poverty. Ashley remembers picking up cans from rubbish bins and the side of the road for money to supplement their meager grocery budget. Food at meals would be rationed between Ashley and her younger sister, with her mother often going without.

Finally, after enduring six years of abuse and deprivation, Lisa Callingbull Ground had had enough. With her boyfriend out of town, Lisa told Ashley to pack a bag. She loaded her two daughters into a pickup truck and headed back to Enoch and the safety of her parents' home. When they arrived in Enoch, Lisa's confusion, pain, and trauma that she had suffered over the years bubbled forth in hysteria. Lisa was unaware of the abuse her daughter had experienced, though, and she was devastated when Ashley shared about her mistreatment. Back in the security of their family, both mother and daughter began the long road to healing, mentally and physically.

With her difficult childhood, Ashley is often asked why she didn't turn to drugs and alcohol. "What I did was turn to my culture. I pushed myself into my culture, into my beliefs and my traditions, and I used that to find myself and to heal."

The move and transition to living in Enoch was not an easy one for Ashley. There were years of legal battles after her family pressed charges against the sex offender. The court hearings led to anxiety and frustration that no teenager should have to endure. Ashley was a damaged, angry young girl who hated herself and suffered a total lack of self-worth that outside therapy could not address. Her trust in people had been destroyed, and she often responded to help by either lashing out or withdrawing from the situation. Her family knew she needed more than modern therapy could provide. She needed the healing she could receive from traditional medicine.

Ashley's grandparents were Wisdom Keepers, knowledgeable in traditional Cree culture and medicine. They helped her reconnect with her culture and spirituality to aid in the healing process. Ashley was able to follow the "red road." In the Cree culture, the red road is the right path of life where one stays away from negative behaviors, such as using drugs and alcohol, in order to have a clean body, spirit, and mind. Her grandparents used traditional medicine to help people with physical ailments and personal problems. Ashley credits them for her survival and the ability to move beyond the pain from the past. She says, "Watching them, I wanted to be like them. I instantly felt so much better embracing that lifestyle because that's who I am." Ashley found peace by emulating the selflessness of her grandparents through volunteering and charity work.

With love and attention showered upon her, Ashley began to heal, thrive, grow strong, and believe in herself. Even from an early age, Ashley realized that education in all forms would be her road to success. Her formal education was enriched with dance training in ballet, jazz, tap, and pointe. Being a bright student, she accelerated through her classes and graduated from high school at the age of sixteen. One of her proudest moments occurred at her high school graduation banquet. She said, "It was my kokum's last wish to see me graduate. She was dying of a lung disease called pulmonary fibrosis, and the only time she left the hospital was to attend my graduation." At the banquet, Ashley performed by singing in Cree and playing the hand drum. She noted, "It was my proudest moment because I got to do something for my kokum before she passed away, and that is something I can always hold dear." After her high school graduation, Ashley continued her education at Northern Alberta Institute of Technology, with a focus on drama, acting, and television.

In addition to her schooling, the influence of her grandparents helped mold her strong belief in service to others by working with charitable organizations and advocating for Indigenous people. Ashley started volunteering for charities at the age of fourteen, around the time her six-day-old sister passed away. The infant had Trisomy 18, a genetic disorder that causes a baby's organs to develop abnormally. Ashley experienced more heartbreak when her grandmother suffered from pulmonary fibrosis and died a year later. These tragedies led to her work with Stollery Children's Hospital Foundation, and she continues to volunteer for other charities, including Run for the Cure (her mother is a breast cancer survivor) and the Canadian Lung Association (Ashley contracted tuberculosis when she was nine, and her beloved grandmother died of lung disease). Her commitment to charity work later became Ashley's motivation to compete in beauty pageants. Others convinced her that joining the pageant world would allow her to pursue her true passion: charity and advocacy work.

Ashley in gold jingle dress regalia.

As a youngster, she competed in many contests. By the age of ten, she had won all the Enoch Cree Nation's princess crowns and later vied for four other national and international titles. There came a point, though, in her early twenties, that the luster had faded from pageant competition. The life was strenuous, both mentally and physically. The demands of constant training, the calorie counting, and the ruthless competitive culture all became too much. The constant stress and blatant prejudice she experienced took its toll. She was the target of cruel, racist remarks, such as being called a "dirty Native Indian," and was the object of vicious jokes when she won the 2010 Miss Canada competition, such as, "I wonder if she's going to drink Lysol for a talent or sign welfare checks with her toes." She stepped away from the pageant world after a few years, moving to the Six Nations reserve where she worked with troubled teens. During this time, she met her future husband, Ryan Burnham, and they were married in February 2015.

The decision to stop competing in pageants, however, was not as easy as one might think. Ashley was being encouraged to compete again by friends who pointed out that the contests could be a good way to support the charities she valued so highly. Months later, her mother contacted her with a possibility that she couldn't ignore. The Mrs. Universe pageant doesn't have a swimsuit component; instead, it prioritizes advocacy and charity work. That year's Mrs. Universe competition had a theme: child abuse and domestic violence. Overcoming the struggles she experienced in her earlier life convinced Ashley that this pageant was an opportunity through which she could truly effect change. She satisfied all the qualifications, and the pageant mission was perfectly suited to her interests. All that was left to do was to fill out the application.

On August 29, 2015, Ashley Callingbull Burnham made history. She became the first Canadian and the first Indigenous woman to win the Mrs. Universe title. She lost no time in acting on the themes of the pageant that year. She knew she would have the attention of the world, and she wanted her first official statements to shine a glaring light on the serious problems that plague Indigenous people. That very night, she packed her bags for a 4:00 a.m. flight home to Canada. "This is the perfect time to open my mouth," she told her husband in the hotel room. "This is the perfect time to tell the truth." And tell the truth she did! Since then, Ashley has been instrumental in bringing issues to the forefront of tribal, provincial, and federal government.

Ashley is a woman of many talents that have brought her to prominence in an array of diverse arenas. She partnered with well-known Native photographer Anthony "Thosh" Collins in 2013 to model for Thosh's Re:appropriation project. This work highlighted the misuse of Native designs and regalia. Determined to squash the stereotypes of Native dress, she rummaged through her grandfather's closet and provided the real Native look. She carried that practice forward to her Mrs. Universe competition when she wore traditional regalia, showcasing the healing dance and wearing a jingle dress.

Ashley has fought hard to bring the terrible crisis of missing and murdered Indigenous women and girls to the attention of every Canadian as well as the world. Ashley lost a relative when she was young (the woman's body was later found buried on a pig farm), which made her a staunch advocate of the cause. In fact, there are many causes that Ashley supports, and she has had a positive impact on all of them: voting rights, education for Native youth, mentorship, and domestic and sexual violence. She has the megaphone and is making her voice heard.

Ashley Callingbull Burnham tells young people, "Never let fear stop you from chasing dreams, because you have no idea of the potential you have inside of you." There are few people who could give that advice with more truth and sincerity. Ashley has managed to overcome incredible adversity and succeed in a world that seemed to have everything stacked against her. She now fills her days by mentoring young people, speaking at youth centers and domestic violence shelters, and traveling as an ambassador for the many charities with which she works. Her greatest satisfaction comes from letting young people know she has felt the pain that many of them carry and that there is a way out of that terror. She says, "I think it's really important to have a role model that's relatable. These kids that I talk to in all these different schools—it's good to open their eyes and show them that they can really push themselves and become successful. Her motto is "Love and live fearlessly," a belief that she lives by and enthusiastically shares with others.

AWARDS AND HONORS

- 50 Influential People: The Movers, the Shakers, and the Difference-Makers award, *Alberta Venture* magazine, 2016
- Mrs. Universe, 2015
- Role Model Award, United Nations, October 2015
- Miss Universe Canada, finalist, 2013
- Top 20 Under 30 Award, Canada, 2012
- Role Model Award, Dreamcatcher Gala, 2011
- Miss Universe Canada, second runner-up, 2010

CHAPTER 2

Henrietta Mann, PhD

SOUTHERN CHEYENNE
Ho'e-osta-oo-nah'e (Prayer Woman)

Even in the worst situations, find the good there, because we also believe that we are here one time. I don't have a second chance to come back and correct anything that I may not have done right.

HENRIETTA MANN

s the spring winds blew across the green prairie grass, the cry of a newborn filled the air. She was the child of Henry and Lenora Wolftongue Mann. Her entry into this world on May 22, 1934, was long awaited and much anticipated by all, especially White Buffalo Woman, her great-grandmother.

To introduce her to the world that lay ahead, White Buffalo Woman held the child in prayer, as she would a sacred pipe, offering her to the four sacred directions, then to the earth, and then to the sky. She named her Standing Twenty Woman, meaning she would have the abilities and knowledge of twenty women. She later told the child's father, as she lay on her deathbed, that Henrietta was the child she had been waiting for. The old Cheyenne woman knew this child would do great things. Henrietta Mann was born, blessed, and on her way to the long life and successful future her great-grandmother had prayed for.

Henrietta, or Henri, as she would be called, was part of a large, loving family that had four generations all living together in a three-room house. She can remember the layout of the house and her great-grandmother's bed tucked away in the kitchen, usually the warmest room in the house. The Mann family lived in a traditional communal arrangement near Hammon, Oklahoma, on land allotted to her grandfather in the 1880s. They raised cattle and lived off the land until the 1950s, when the Cheyenne people were forced to move into towns or to government lands nearby.

Living in a multigenerational household meant there was never a shortage of love for young Henrietta. When she and her father would drive up to their house, she would jump out of the car before it came to a complete stop and run into the arms of her great-grandmother. One of her fondest memories growing up is crawling onto her great-grandmother's lap for an embrace from that strong woman who had suffered so much in her life.

Henri's great-grandmothers, White Buffalo Woman and Vister, survived two separate attacks on Chief Black Kettle's Cheyenne people by US troops: the massacres at Sand Creek in 1864 and at Washita in 1868. Between the two attacks, nearly three hundred Cheyenne people were killed and mutilated or taken captive for slaves. Colonel Chivington, who led the Sand Creek slaughter, let loose the following battle cry as his troops descended on the camp at dawn while the villagers slept: "Damn any man who sympathizes with Indians. Kill and scalp them all, big and little; nits make lice."

Such tragic memories are the history of Native people. They can make a person resentful and angry, but they also can make a person stronger and more determined. The latter was the case with Henri Mann. The Mann family valued their his-

Henrietta Mann.

tory, language, and culture, and Henri credits her grandfather for this. He was her first and dearest friend and the one who made sure she was raised with the knowledge of the Cheyenne culture and language. Once Henri started school, her grandfather would have an aunt come to the house every afternoon and teach her the Cheyenne language.

Henri was a good student, even as a very young girl. She had a passion for learning, and she begged her mother to start school early. Living under the authority of the government's Indian agent, her parents needed permission for this to happen. The agent gave his approval for Henri to begin school early but demonstrated the open prejudice shown toward Native people at the time. He told her parents that she'd get tired of school soon enough and they could take her out then. He was hinting that she was not bright enough to handle the rigors of formal education, but those comments made Henrietta even more determined to learn.

As Henri progressed through school, she often experienced blatant discrimination that caused hurt and sometimes anger. When her teacher would ask the students to name colors or count to one hundred, little hands would shoot up, Native and non-Native alike, but never would the Native children be called upon. The most hurtful was when the Native children were routinely segregated from the rest of the class to be checked for lice. These practices, carried out by teachers and other adults, caused the white children to call the Native students names such as "lousy Indian" or "dirty Indian." The pain and humiliation were too much at times for young Henri, and she voiced her upset to her grandfather. He shared his wisdom with her and explained, "They look at us differently, and you will have to deal with what Indian-Anglo relations are all about. Your great-grandmother prayed for you to lead a good life. Always remain Cheyenne and try to make them better people." Henrietta Mann says, "And that is why I decided to become a teacher."

Henrietta enjoyed school and advanced very quickly. After graduating at the age of seventeen from Hammon High School, she received a scholarship to attend Southwestern Oklahoma State University. She graduated in 1954 with a bachelor's degree in English with a minor in business education and was the first Cheyenne woman to receive a college degree. Henri was living up to her name of Standing Twenty Woman. She had shown her knowledge and determination to succeed. At this time her family honored her with a new name, Prayer Woman, after her paternal grandmother, Lucy Whitebear Mann.

Over the next sixteen years, Henrietta and her husband, Al Whiteman, along with their four children, experienced a series of changes and challenges. Henri's first teaching position was on the other side of the country in Barstow, California, worlds away from her family in Oklahoma. She taught English, social studies, and typing classes to middle school and high school students. The years were filled with the usual responsibilities of raising a family and working on an advanced degree. She completed her master's degree in 1970 at Oklahoma State University and was immediately hired at the University of California, Berkeley, where she taught courses in Native American studies.

What an exciting time it was in Berkeley! The United States was experiencing terrible social upheaval, and protests and demonstrations were a constant occurrence. The African American Black Panthers group and Native American organizations, such as the American Indian Movement, were voicing their frustration over social injustice. Although Henrietta was teaching Native American studies, her classes were often a sea of white faces. The Native students were gone, as they had joined the protests taking over Alcatraz, the abandoned federal prison located in the San Francisco Bay. This did not daunt Henri's enthusiasm for teaching, though. She says, "I felt inspired to share our wonderful Native ways with the students, the majority of whom were non-Natives. I said to myself, 'This is where I belong.'" And that is where she stayed for the next two years. But with a growing family and unrest often on every corner, Henrietta and Al decided this was not a healthy environment in which to raise their children. They made the decision to move to Missoula, Montana, where Henri had been offered a directorship and faculty position at the University of Montana.

Teaching at the university level is demanding. Although it is always rewarding, it is never without challenges. Soon Henri realized that if she wanted to excel in higher education, she would have to get her doctorate degree (PhD). It was time for another move. The University of New Mexico was her next stop, and in 1982 she completed her doctorate degree. This happened at a time when very few Native Americans had college degrees, much less a doctorate. She continued her teaching at the University of Montana, but other opportunities lay ahead.

After nearly twenty-eight years at the University of Montana, Henri was ready for a change. When people are part of an organization for so long, they sometimes become like the chairs at a table—they are expected to always be there. But Henrietta's self-described personality as a "boat rocker" created opportunity, and she forged ahead. She uprooted and moved to Montana State University, where she became the first Katz Endowed Chair in the Native American Studies department. The endowed chair position was created from a generous donation of $1.25 million to the university that would forever fund the salary of this position.

Henrietta's time at Montana State University has been a kaleidoscope of activities: from teacher, to assistant to the president, to becoming an internationally renowned speaker on education, Native American culture, and the environment. No matter what challenge Henri takes on, be assured that it will be focused on her passion: education for the improvement of the Native American people.

Henrietta Mann was born of humble beginnings, blessed by her great-grandmother, and has lived in the Cheyenne way. The years have made Henrietta's life a scrapbook of happiness and joy, full of loves and losses. On the day she was accepted into her doctoral program, her husband lost his fight with liver disease and passed away. Years later, her son and brother died of alcohol abuse. Life can challenge the heart and spirit, but Henrietta reaches back to the words of her ancestors and says, "Those kinds of losses are tragic. They can make you a very bitter, jaded individual. I hope I'm not that way. There is beauty in tragedy. Life is what we make of it."

This powerful Cheyenne woman has been a teacher, mentor, role model, and spiritual guide. Henri credits her family for the value they put on education and the culture of the Cheyenne people. She is a strong advocate for the environment and proud to represent Native people in their belief that all have a responsibility to love and protect our mother, the earth. Henri's work as a teacher has taken place in classrooms and conference halls, but she has never forgotten to live and teach the Cheyenne way. She says, "Our time on Earth is very short. We should be about love and respect. Not one of us has a corner on sacredness. We should recognize each other as children of Mother Earth and Father Sky, recognize kinship, recognize different cultures, different ways of looking at life." These words have changed the lives Henrietta Mann has touched and will continue to change lives into the future.

AWARDS AND HONORS

- Oklahoma House of Representatives, House Concurrent Resolution 1014, which commends Dr. Mann for her distinguished career in teaching Native American studies, furthering the educational opportunities for members of American Indian tribes, and being a strong advocate for the preservation of American Indian culture, 2020
- National Academy of Education, elected member for distinguished merit, 2016
- Lifetime Achievement Award, Native American Student Advocacy Institute, 2013
- Legacy Award Winner, Working Mother Media, 2009
- Lifetime Achievement Award, National Indian Education Association, 2009
- Bernard S. Rody Award, University of New Mexico Alumni Association, 2008

- Cheyenne and Arapaho Tribal College, founding president, 2008
- Katz Endowed Chair, first recipient, Montana State University, 2003
- Inductee, Distinguished Alumni Hall of Fame, Southwestern Oklahoma State University, 1997
- Appeared in the Ken Burns PBS documentary *The West* as interviewee and cultural guide, 1996
- Featured as one of five twentieth-century women educators, National Women's History Project, 1995
- Honor Roll of Ten Top Professors Nationwide, *Rolling Stone* magazine, 1991
- National American Indian Woman of the Year, American Indian Heritage Foundation, 1988

Ruth Anna Buffalo

MANDAN, HIDATSA, AND ARIKARA NATION
Mia Eh'Desh (Woman Appears)

I believe in wanting to make change for our future generations. We really need to focus on our youth and listen to our youth.

RUTH ANNA BUFFALO

Growing up Indigenous and growing up on an Indian reservation entails struggles and challenges that most non–Native Americans cannot grasp. The poverty and isolation can sometimes cause a person to give in or give up, and lead them to believe there is no reason to keep trying to do better. Ruth Anna Buffalo was born in Watford City, North Dakota, in August 1977 and was given her grandmother's Native name, Woman Appears. She grew up on the Fort Berthold Indian Reservation in the rural western part of the state. Ruth remembers following the dirt path behind her house into the rugged North Dakota badlands. She swam in creeks edged with beaver dams, searched for artifacts, and hiked the hillsides overlooking Lake Sakakawea. For her and her siblings, the lake and the land around it were places filled with adventure.

Ruth's maternal grandfather, though, looked at the lake with sadness. It was created by the US Army Corps of Engineers when the Garrison Dam was built in the 1950s. When

Ruth Anna Buffalo in the North Dakota House of Representatives chambers.

it was finished, the dam flooded a large portion of the Fort Berthold Indian Reservation and swallowed up his town of Elbowoods. Families were forced to leave their homes for higher ground. Strong opposition to this dam came from those who lived on the banks of the Missouri River, primarily Native Americans, who were forced to abandon their homes and livelihoods when the waters rose to create Lake Sakakawea. This action caused a splintering of the Three Affiliated Tribes—the Mandan, Hidatsa, and Arikara Nation (MHA Nation)—which lived on the Fort Berthold Indian Reservation. These tribes were made up of farmers and ranchers, and the land was their livelihood. They knew how to live off the land and supported their families well. But with the building of the dam, all that was lost (96 percent of the reservation land is now underwater). This forced many members in this Indigenous community to leave the reservation to find work. Ruth's family was one that suffered the loss of their homeland. Her grandfather left their home in search of work, and he eventually changed his Native name to improve his chances of getting hired for jobs in the city. Ruth's grandmother helped support the family by creating and selling her exceptional beadwork and crafts.

Ruth Buffalo came from a strong matrilineal heritage, which means their legacy is passed down through the mother's side of the family and the children are members of the mother's clan. Ruth's mother, Maxine Bolman Buffalo, was a single mother who raised Ruth and her three younger sisters on her own. Maxine was also a loving and compassionate woman who believed in the value of a strong family unit. In addition to her biological children, Maxine adopted and raised two of Ruth's older cousins, as well as her own three brothers.

Growing up on the reservation is challenging, and one of the main reasons why is the overt discrimination faced by Native people, even when they are young. Ruth Buffalo remembers attending church in a town that borders the Fort Berthold Indian Reservation. After services, the four-year-old girl and her mother went to the church basement for the coffee-and-donuts type of gathering that is normally held. The priest chatted with them briefly and then, after he learned that the woman and girl were from the reservation, told them they should go home. The little girl and her mom got up from the table and left.

Ruth found racial prejudice in many aspects of life on the reservation. Sometimes it was a benign hurtful gesture, but other times it could be life-threatening. When Ruth was ten years old, her younger sister was misdiagnosed at the local health clinic in Mandaree, the town where her family lived. The young girl had appendicitis, which meant that her appendix was on the verge of rupturing and could threaten her life. When Ruth's mother brought the young girl to the clinic, the health-care providers turned them away. They said the girl just had flu-like symptoms and told her mother to take the child home and give her Tylenol. But Ruth's mother did not do as she was told. Instead, she drove the little girl twenty-seven miles to Watford City, the nearest town that had a hospital. The ambulance rushed her to the next level of care in Williston, where she had surgery and recovered from that serious medical emergency.

Inequity, discrimination, and prejudice can leave lasting, debilitating scars, especially on young minds, and can often affect a person well into adulthood. But it's also possible to grow from these experiences, rise above the hurt, and apply that learning to positive life work, which is just what Ruth did. Through self-motivation and the influence of strong role models, she was determined to make a difference in this world.

Following that frightening event with her sister, Ruth set her mind on becoming a medical doctor. She attended a summer program starting in the seventh grade that included physics, chemistry, and math. These six-week programs occupied her summers until she took premedical classes in college. In her senior year, she encountered a turning point: Ruth discovered that she was unable to work with cadavers. This stark realization meant that she had to make a life-changing decision, one that ended up altering her career path.

Although medical school was not in her future, Ruth committed herself to the health-care field and advocated for the wellness and dignity of all people. She attended Si Tanka University in South Dakota and earned a bachelor's degree in criminal justice. After college graduation, Ruth took a job as a substance-abuse prevention coordinator for her tribe. She went on to work for seven years at the United Tribes Techni-

Swearing-in day in the North Dakota House chambers.

cal College as a strengthening lifestyles director. Having been a star on her college basketball team, she was abundantly qualified when she became the head women's basketball coach as well as the men's assistant basketball coach. Ruth was the first woman in the college's history to serve on both coaching staffs.

In 2011, Ruth won a Susan G. Komen Foundation scholarship to study public health at the University of Kansas Medical Center. She became a member of a breast cancer research team and, from there, went on to complete three master's degrees: one in public health, one in management, and one in business administration. That ten-year-old girl who almost lost her little sister due to prejudice in the medical field was now positioned to make a difference in health care and the treatment of Native people.

Throughout her life, Ruth Buffalo has never been afraid to volunteer. She has served on a multitude of boards and commissions, such as the National Education for Women's Leadership Institute, to hone her skills. About that experience, she states, "I feel like that planted a seed for me." The program gave her the training to gain practical leadership knowledge. Its focus was on empowering underrepresented voices in the community, particularly for women of color, low-income women, and women with disabilities. After completing this program, Ruth was ready to pursue her biggest challenge yet—running for a legislative seat in the North Dakota state legislature. She ran, and she won.

Ruth worked hard to get elected as a state representative. Being Native American, she fought the odds and was elected in a district that is less than 1 percent American Indian/Alaska Native and is 90 percent white. Ruth's election was a huge upset, considering the population and cultural conservatism of the state. She became the first female Native American Democrat elected to the North Dakota Legislative Assembly. The path she took in life led her to the North Dakota House of Representatives, where her influence will have a lasting effect on the lives of all the people she serves in her state and beyond.

Ruth is deeply passionate about voting rights for Native Americans as well as preventing violence against women. She is particularly concerned about the alarming number of missing and murdered Indigenous women. Her election to the state House of Representatives was impressive on many levels, especially because she did it by unseating the primary sponsor of the voter ID law in North Dakota. This bill specifically stated that in order to be allowed to vote in elections, a person must present identification with a street address displayed. If this law had passed, it would have prevented the vast majority of Native Americans in North Dakota from voting. That's because people who live on Indian reservations seldom have street addresses and only use post office boxes. Mail is rarely delivered directly to houses on sprawling Indian reservation lands. Another concern with the bill was that it could have set a dangerous precedent for other states to follow. With Ruth's successful campaign, the threat of Native American voter suppression was voted down.

The crisis of physical and sexual abuse of Native women is not new, but recent years have seen an upsurge in advocacy for the cause. Ruth Buffalo has fought diligently to put an end to the horrific problem of human trafficking, violence toward women, and murdered and missing Indigenous women and girls. Upon being elected in 2018, Ruth sponsored and successfully passed six bills advocating that legislative action be taken to address these issues. Since 1885, there have been laws related to policing on tribal lands that generally limited tribal authority. In 2013, the Violence Against Women Act expanded tribal jurisdiction to include some violent crimes, but it still didn't cover sexual violence or human trafficking.

In areas where tribes don't have jurisdiction, either the FBI or county sheriffs are supposed to provide support, depending on the state. Unfortunately, that doesn't always happen. The sheriff's departments in some states and the FBI in others

Representative Buffalo with US Representative Deb Haaland.

are understaffed and underfunded, and the negative fallout from this is evident. According to a Government Accountability Office report, between 2005 and 2009, federal prosecutors declined to prosecute 67 percent of the 2,500 cases in Indian Country involving sexual violence that were referred to them. This is the injustice that Ruth Buffalo is determined to fight. She states, "I was invited to testify before the House Subcommittee on Indigenous Peoples of the United States to address the growing rates of missing and murdered Indigenous women in our country. This is a crisis I do not take lightly."

Ruth takes pride in her Native American heritage and its powerful connection to its people and the land. She comes from a long line of women leaders, with her grandmother and mother being strong community advocates. Many other family members served in the US military. Through her volunteerism and work as a state representative, Ruth hopes to help heal communities by reconnecting Native youth to their land, culture, and language. This includes never giving up on working together, lifting up the young people, and staying connected with the elders. Ruth says, "Find ways to help for the greater good, and thread the needle toward justice for everyone."

Standing alongside other newly elected lawmakers during the swearing-in ceremony, Ruth Buffalo wore a traditional Native American dress and held an eagle feather fan given to her by her clan brothers hours earlier. "Eagle feathers in our culture are very significant. Oftentimes they're gifted to people when they've accomplished a great achievement." Ruth went on to explain that the traditional clothing is part of her identity and that wearing it to her swearing-in ceremony was a way to pay tribute to her community, honor her ancestors, and promote the value of Native culture for future generations.

AWARDS AND HONORS

- Kroc Institute for Peace and Justice Fellowship, 2019–2020
- North Dakota Democratic–NonPartisan League, secretary, 2017
- Fargo Native American Commission appointee, 2016
- National Center for American Indian Enterprise Development 40 under 40 award, 2016
- Fargo, North Dakota, Hall of Fame inductee, 2015
- The North Dakota Women's Business Center, a program of the Center for Technology & Business (now CBT), Women's Leadership Program, 2015
- Komen Scholar, Susan G. Komen Foundation scholarship recipient, 2011
- Business Watch 40 under 40 recipient, *Bismarck Tribune*, 2010

CHAPTER 4

Elouise Pepion Cobell

BLACKFEET
Inokesquetee saki (Yellow Bird Woman)

Anytime you have movement that seeks fundamental change for a longstanding injustice, there always has to be an iconic figure who leads the charge, the person who refuses to go to the back of the bus. That person is Elouise.

KEITH HARPER, A LEAD ATTORNEY ON THE COBELL CASE

louise Pepion Cobell was bigger than life. She was a force of nature who saw an injustice and set forth to correct the inequity. She took on the United States government and won—big-time. She sued for the mismanagement of five hundred thousand individual Native American accounts handled by the US Bureau of Indian Affairs (BIA). Elouise dedicated fifteen years of her life to resolving the lawsuit, which resulted in a $3.4 billion settlement.

This remarkable woman came from the humblest of beginnings. Elouise was born on the Blackfeet Indian Reservation on November 5, 1945, to Polite Lawrence Pepion and Catherine Dubray. Elouise was the great-granddaughter of the revered Blackfeet leader Mountain Chief, who led his people first on the battlefield and then in negotiations in Washington, DC, in the 1850s. Elouise's parents raised her to be a strong woman, and, like Mountain Chief, her determination also took her to Washington, DC, to fight for her people.

Elouise was the seventh of nine children in the Pepion family. They grew up on the windswept prairie of Montana in a home that had no running water or electricity. Their father raised cattle and grew hay to feed the cows, while the children were all expected to work on the ranch. When Elouise was asked where she got the stamina to keep moving forward despite the setbacks she often experienced later in life, she would share what her mother told her: "'I didn't raise any weak women. I only raised strong women.' And so we remembered not to run away and say, 'Poor me, poor me.' We were standing up and being strong."

Growing up on an Indian reservation in the 1950s meant that local schooling was not available. Elouise's older sisters and brothers were sent away to attend government-run Indian boarding schools. These schools were part of the US government's strategy to educate Native Americans to fit into the "more acceptable" white community. They were designed to teach Native children the values and knowledge of the dominant white society while keeping them away from the traditional Native lifestyle of their families. These schools were located long distances away from their homes, which made it impossible for them to see their families during the school year. This nine-month or longer separation was very difficult on both the children and their parents.

President Obama meets Elouise Cobell.

When Elouise was four years old, her father managed to get a one-room schoolhouse built so that children in the area would not have to go away to boarding school. She recalled visiting the new school with her father, sitting down at one of the desks, and refusing to leave until she was allowed to attend. She went to school there until she left for high school, which was fifty miles away. That one-room schoolhouse exposed her to the world outside the reservation. "It opened my eyes," she recalled, "and made me want to do a lot of things."

Throughout her years of education, Elouise was a good student and, in particular, was skilled in working with numbers, also known as ciphering. When she graduated from high school, Elouise attended Great Falls Commercial College and Montana State University, where she studied accounting. While attending the university, she interned as a clerk at the Blackfeet Bureau of Indian Affairs office. Her job as an intern helped pay for college, but, more importantly, it was where she saw firsthand the negligence and injustice shown toward Native people, something she'd often heard about when she was growing up.

As a child, Elouise would listen to her parents and their friends complain about the Bureau of Indian Affairs and its management of their property. Like hundreds of thousands of Indians across the country, they owned rights to land held in trust by the federal government. "In trust" meant that the government leased or handled all the business dealings for the Native Americans who owned the property. This included arranging for companies to use Native land for oil drilling, livestock grazing, or timber logging. The BIA leased the land on the Native owner's behalf and was supposed to give the owner checks for the payments due.

Young Elouise would stand in her backyard and watch the white men who were doing business on her father's land. There were riggers pumping oil, cattlemen grazing herds, and lumberjacks harvesting trees. Whatever money they were obviously making was not going to the Cobell family, however. Elouise recalled her father saying, "Why am I not getting anything? It's my land."

While working that first job with the BIA, Elouise realized the answer to her father's question. She remembered, with much frustration, how people would come to the BIA office to pick up the checks they were owed. They would wait, sitting on hard wooden benches, sometimes all day or longer, while the agent sat behind a teller window ignoring them. Once, Elouise went into the agent's office to tell him to help the people, but she found him asleep. She recalled stories told by her relatives about an aunt who was desperate for her lease check because her husband was very ill. She caught a ride on a horse-drawn wagon to the Blackfeet agency, where several people were already waiting outside in chest-deep snow. Finally, an official came out and told them to come back tomorrow. Her aunt had to ask people for a place to stay overnight. When she returned the next day, she was told that the checks would not be ready for another two weeks. In fact, they did not arrive until the following spring. Elouise's uncle died shortly after the checks arrived.

These stories that Elouise heard from family and friends made her question why. Why were Native Americans treated so poorly? How could the US government get away with not providing lease payments and other support that was legally due the Native people? These were questions that spurred Elouise to demand accountability from the government.

Education was important to the Cobell family, as demonstrated by Elouise's father when he helped get that one-room schoolhouse built near their home. Elouise pursued education as a means to an end—the path to righting the wrongs she had observed over the years. She was well on her way to a degree in accounting at Montana State University when she was notified that her mother was very sick. Elouise said that her mother begged her to stay in school, but family is sacred in Native American tradition and elders are to be taken care of. Her mother needed her, and she wanted to be by her side. Catherine Pepion passed away in 1968, but Elouise never returned to the university. Instead, she set off on her own to "see that world outside the reservation" that she had dreamed of as a four-year-old in that one-room schoolhouse.

Elouise moved to Seattle, Washington, and pursued a job in the field that she loved, working in accounting at a local television station. The city exposed her to a life and experiences she did not have in her Montana home. During this time, she met Alvin Cobell, another Blackfeet Indian who worked on fishing boats in Alaska. They were married and had their only child, a son named Turk.

In 1971, Elouise made another decision based on the needs of her family, setting her on a path that would shape the rest of her days. Her brother was seriously injured and left paralyzed, and there was no one to help her father on the family ranch. The Cobell family left Seattle and moved back to Montana to help Elouise's father run the Blacktail Ranch, which had fallen on hard times. Elouise recalled, "Once we got on that ranch, there was no going back. We just wanted to make sure we held on to our land, and that nobody would take it from us."

Drawing on her upbringing and education, Elouise used the versatility of her background to approach the many challenges that life presented during the next few years. A rancher at heart, she worked with her husband tending baby calves in the spring, growing and baling hay in the summer, and feeding cows in the winter. Their priority was getting the ranch on good footing financially and maintaining it that way.

Elouise and her family settled into their new home and adjusted to rural life. Her husband, Alvin, was happy being back in the country. He was hunting and fishing like he did growing up, which helped put food on the table. They were busy raising a new son and were working hard on the ranch. As in many small communities, the Cobells' return to the reservation did not go unnoticed, and in 1976, the Blackfeet tribal officials asked Elouise to become the treasurer for the tribe.

Accepting the position offered to her by the tribal leaders meant that Elouise would be responsible for the accounts of thousands of tribal members who leased their property to outside companies. Reflecting on her experience seventeen or so years back while working in the BIA offices, she was aware of the attitudes held by some employees concerning accountability to the Native people. As Elouise became more familiar with the duties of her job, she realized that the span of years did not see any improvement in the BIA practices. Again, she found herself at odds with the BIA on their accounting procedures and questioned why tribal members' accounts were often not credited the income they were due. The BIA officials told her that she should learn to read a financial statement. Humiliated but undeterred, she kept tracking discrepancies and asking for explanations.

For twenty years, Elouise worked for the betterment of the Blackfeet people, with much of that time devoted to fighting the Bureau of Indian Affairs over errors and inconsistencies, either with tribal affairs or individual accounts. In violation of federal law, the BIA often failed to invest money to gain interest on it. Sometimes the agency lost the Native landowner's money but officials would ignore the error, waiting for the individual to complain before correcting the mistake. The money in Blackfeet accounts was often used as a BIA slush fund to loan to other tribes, and then the bureau would just "forget" to replace it. Another misuse of funds happened when the US government allowed Indian trust funds to be used for New York City's 1975 fiscal crisis, the 1979 Chrysler car company's bailout, and the reduction of the US national debt.

These findings and others motivated Elouise to call senators, federal officials, and anyone else who would listen, but she got no results. She contacted financial officers from other tribes and determined that the Blackfeet Nation was not alone in having serious problems with BIA accounting. After years of trying to work with the BIA, she decided it was time to take another approach. Elouise and four other financial officers filed a lawsuit, *Cobell v. Norton*. This was the first step in what would become the largest government settlement ever awarded in the history of the United States.

On June 10, 1996, Elouise, along with the Native American Rights Fund and lead attorney Dennis Gingold, filed the lawsuit against the United States Department of the Interior. Their complaint did not demand money damages, even though they estimated that the United States owed the Native people billions of dollars. They just wanted an accounting of the funds. Where was the money and what was it used for?

The lawsuit dragged on. The government lawyers tried to thwart the case at every turn. The legal battle spanned fifteen years, four administrations, ten legal appeals, thirty-six hundred court filings, and the unprecedented action of a federal judge being removed from the case because he was seen by the government's lawyers as too biased for the plaintiffs (the Cobells' side). It finally ended in late 2010 when Congress passed legislation that was signed by President Barack Obama. A federal judge gave final approval on June 20, 2011. The settlement was $3.4 billion for the mismanagement of funds, tribal land purchases, and a higher education scholarship fund named for Elouise Cobell. The fight was over, and Elouise Cobell had won.

Elouise was a humble yet powerful woman who liked to joke about having made the leap from being a "dumb Indian" to "genius" in one lifetime after she won a coveted MacArthur Foundation "genius grant". Her life was a kaleidoscope of constant motion, and the famous legal victory was only one frame of that moving picture. Elouise dedicated her life to righting the injustice that she saw directed toward Native American people. She saw the younger generation as the hope of her work being carried on. Her contributions were many, including helping launch the first Native American bank and starting the Blackfeet's mini bank that taught students financial information and how to set up savings accounts with the local Blackfeet-owned bank.

After the final legislative bill was signed, Turk Cobell stated, "My mother is tremendously relentless when it comes to doing what she believes is right. Maybe now she can finally enjoy a normal life again and get something she hasn't had: rest." Unfortunately, that was not to be for Elouise. She died of cancer on October 16, 2011, just six months after the signing ceremony for the bill. Although Elouise was unable to savor her accomplishments for long, she recognized the importance of her work. She said, "First they ignore you, then they laugh at you, then they fight you, then you win." Words that brought her satisfaction to the end.

AWARDS AND HONORS

- National Native American Hall of Fame inductee, 2018
- "100 Years: One Woman's Fight for Justice," a seventy-five-minute documentary, Melinda Janko, 2016
- Presidential Medal of Freedom presented by President Barack Obama; her son, Turk Cobell, accepted the medal on her behalf, 2016
- Dartmouth College, honorary degree of doctor of humane letters, 2011
- Montana Trial Lawyers Association's Citizens Award, 2011
- Impact Award, American Association of Retired Persons, 2007
- Rural Heroes Award, National Rural Assembly, 2007
- Cultural Freedom Fellowship, Lannan Foundation, 2005
- Jay Silverheels Achievement Award, National Center for American Indian Enterprise Development, 2004
- Montana State University, honorary doctorate, 2002
- Women Who Make a Difference Award, International Women's Forum, 2002
- Genius grant, John D. and Catherine T. MacArthur Foundation's Fellowship Program, 1997

Loriene Roy, PhD

ANISHINABE, WHITE EARTH RESERVATION

Let us put our minds together and see what life we will make for our children.

SITTING BULL, LAKOTA

As the car pulled away from the house, she turned to look out the passenger-side window to watch the tears and waving hands disappear into the distance. Loriene Roy was setting off, traveling down one of the many roads of her life, roads that would take her to being recognized as an international educator and the leader of the oldest and largest library organization in the world, the American Library Association (ALA). The mission of the ALA is "to provide leadership . . . in order to enhance learning and ensure access to information for all." Loriene's life has been a constant reflection on the importance of learning and education as she has wended her way through her very active years.

Traveling to seek a better way of life was not alien to Loriene or her family. When her father returned to the reservation after serving in the Korean War, he and his new bride planned to follow the US government's encouragement to relocate to a larger city. The Indian Relocation Act of 1956 offered to pay moving expenses and provide some vocational training

Young Loriene in Minnesota.

for those willing to move from the reservations to cities, where employment opportunities were thought to be more favorable. Francis David Roy and Judith Elaine (LaFriniere) Roy were both members of the White Earth Reservation of the Anishinabe (Ojibwe/Chippewa) and were headed for Milwaukee, Wisconsin. A short stopover in Cloquet, Minnesota, to see Francis's sister derailed those plans forever. Loriene's parents decided to settle down in the area. They bought a house in Carlton, a rural town bordering the Fond du Lac Reservation in northern Minnesota, and raised a large, happy family. They adjusted to their new surroundings with little trouble, despite a petition that was circulated to "get the Indians out of town." Being the only Native American family in Carlton was a stark reminder of the overt prejudices toward Native people that prevailed at that time.

Born on June 12, 1954, Loriene was the eldest of eight children. Like her parents, she is Anishinabe, enrolled in the White Earth Reservation, a member of the Minnesota Chippewa tribe, Pembina band and the Makwa ("Bear") Clan. Loriene says, "I have lived a life of survival through good fortune, community service, and hard work." The Roy children had fine role models to learn from. Although neither of Loriene's parents completed high school, they worked hard to instill in their children the value of education, respect for those around them, and the importance of contributing to their community. Loriene's father exemplified these values through his work as a school custodian and bus driver while serving Carlton as a volunteer firefighter, ambulance driver, and mayor. Loriene's mother worked at the nearby match factory and later, as the family grew, became a stay-at-home mom.

When he was in his early fifties, Loriene's father had a stroke and became disabled. Loriene's mother cared for her husband at home for sixteen years. Determined to provide for her family, Judith Roy completed her general equivalency diploma (GED), which certifies that the test taker has high school–level academic skills. She worked as a security guard and then as an Indian education aide at the high school, which is the position she retired from.

Loriene has always had great respect for her parents. She says, "Theirs is a story of strength through good humor and Native pride. This is the legacy that I have tried to continue throughout my life as an educator, public servant, and Indigenous person." These words were spoken with the sincerity that has been the driving force throughout Loriene's life. Growing up, Loriene enjoyed school and loved to read and write. In fact, as early as the first grade, she was writing stories about horses and the world around her. Sometimes she got into arguments with her sister Della about who wrote the story first!

Loriene's love for reading often caused concern for her mother, who did not like her daughter separating herself from the rest of the family to curl up with her favorite book. Loriene's determination to keep books in her daily life led her to a compromise with her mother. She could sit in a corner of the kitchen, in the shadow of the big white freezer, and read to her heart's content, while still being a part of the family as they carried on their conversations around the table. Perhaps this was one of the earliest signs of Loriene's connection to her Makwa ("Bear") Clan's belief in being a mediator or negotiator. Her ability to broker a deal with her mother at a young age proved successful in allowing her to pursue her love of books.

Roy family at Tompson Dam.

Loriene's primary and secondary education were completed in Carlton. She enjoyed school and was a good student. It was during this time that both her mother and father shared many words to live by, advice that Loriene practices to this day. This included respecting others so they, too, might have a chance to shine, or, as her mother would say, "If you know the answer, then someone else does too. Let them answer. Don't always put yourself first." This is a rare trait at a time when people often feel they have the most to say and must be the loudest to demonstrate their intelligence.

Loriene graduated from high school near the top of her class and was eager to pursue a college education. After attending classes at the College of Saint Benedict in Minnesota, Loriene's life led her west to a small rural town in southern Oregon. The area surrounding Klamath Falls was beautiful. She could look out her windows and see majestic Mount Shasta in the distance and experience the four seasons of the Pacific Northwest. But her time in Oregon was not without some of the racial challenges her family had faced when they first moved to Carlton many years before. Being ignored for service at the post office or having issues with her wash at the local laundromat brought back painful memories of the mistreatment of Native Americans.

The move to Oregon was a lonely time for Loriene. Having come from a large family, she found that it was difficult being away from her siblings. She recalls frequently packing a box of goodies to send to her brothers and sisters, which also illustrates the loving care for children that is prevalent in Native American homes.

True to her can-do attitude, Loriene quickly found her footing and was able to take advantage of the resources around her. The Oregon Institute of Technology was located in Klamath Falls, which gave her the opportunity to complete a bachelor's degree in allied health. This would influence her in years to come during her term as the ALA president.

But time marches on and interests change through personal life experiences. After working for a few years in the field of allied health, Loriene started questioning her job satisfaction. It was then that her curiosity and constant desire to learn put her on the path of librarianship. She felt that working with people and understanding their reading interests and information needs would be better aligned with her love of learning than the daily routine of a medical technician. She packed her bags and left Oregon to pursue the degrees that would determine her future career in libraries. She attended the University of Arizona and earned a master's in library science. Loriene later stated, "The decision to get a PhD was similarly fortuitous. There was a scholarship available at the University of Illinois at Urbana-Champaign, and I was the stand-in for the person who had to turn it down." With diplomas in hand, she was positioned to pursue a career that would provide the interest, challenges, and fulfillment she sought.

Loriene became a librarian at the Yuma City County Library District in Yuma, Arizona, but moved into university library work after she finished her PhD. Since 1987, she's been on the faculty at the University of Texas School of Information at Austin. In her classes, students engage in community involvement, getting hands-on experience by designing and providing services for and with organizations and institutions, such as rural public libraries, small academic libraries, and libraries serving tribal communities.

Throughout her years of teaching thousands of students and preparing them to enter the world of library and information science, Loriene has never forgotten the lessons she learned from her parents and from being Anishinabe. Remembering back to when her father would tell his children to "get involved, join, get active" makes her realize how those words ingrained in her the value of community participation and giving back. In her early years, Loriene resisted her father's advice, but now she shares those very words with her students when they ask for guidance. She believes in the value of contributing to her profession and readily states that involvement is the key. "I got involved with ALA as a student member. Gain practical experience while you're a student. Attend events where you can meet library workers. Seek opportunities." Her advice includes planning coursework so that students can gain useful skills that can be offered to employers in the workplace. Although her words are directed toward library workers, they offer sound advice for anyone who is traveling the road to success.

Loriene was elected president of the ALA in 2007. She was the first Native American to lead one of the largest professional organizations in the world, with more than sixty thousand members. Loriene won the election by a landslide. She shared in her inaugural speech that if she were to pick a word for the evening, it would be *sueno*, which means "dream" in her Anishinabe language. She says, "The Anishinabe people are dreamers and predictors. Dreamers are acknowledged, and young people are encouraged to find their dreams and their guardians." During her campaign, Loriene

Loriene with Congressman John Lewis and Dr. Min Chou, Chicago, 2017.

outlined three main concerns: supporting literacy, promoting library information science education through practice, and creating programs for workplace wellness. With her leadership role in the American Library Association, Loriene was in a position to effect change.

Loriene drew upon her life experiences when establishing and successfully accomplishing her goals. Growing up Native American drove home the need to address the literacy problems related to cultural issues and the lack of resources. And, as a former allied health worker, Loriene had an opportunity to work with people and their health concerns. To address these, she formed "working circles" instead of traditional task forces, striving to bring more people into the activities and decision-making process. Always the teacher, she brought current and past students into the work with her, giving them opportunities to learn and grow.

As successful as Loriene's year was as ALA president, it was not without challenges. Midway through her presidency, she was accused of censorship concerning comments she made on the children's book *The Education of Little Tree*. Many questioned the book's content and the authenticity of the author. Controversy over the book still remains. With regard to the lessons she's learned over the years, Loriene says, "One is to face your fears or deficiencies. Another is that many people have ideas for you, but only a few are willing to step up and really help. Keep those people happy!"

Loriene believes her success is due to the strong value system she learned from her parents and others around her. The role models in her life have taught Loriene the value of keeping in touch with people. She had professors who encouraged her to be strong and stand on her own. Most importantly, she sees her son as the best role model of all, as he is a kind, thoughtful, and attentive person to everyone.

The exceptional contributions Loriene has made over the years cover a wide range of areas: education, the advocacy of Indigenous people, the promotion of wellness at home and in the workplace, and the support of literacy programs that

Loriene at the International Indigenous Librarians Forum, Norway, 2011.

bring magic into the lives of all who can read. Projects Loriene initiated that still have a profound impact include If I Can Read, I Can Do Anything, a reading promotion program for Native children on or near reservations. It delivered more than $100,000 in new books to tribal schools and community libraries, provided children with reading incentives, and supported library initiatives, such as family reading nights and an annual writing and art contest. Then there is the Honoring Generations project, which provides scholarships for Native American students interested in tribal librarianship, allowing them to enroll in a program at the University of Texas School of Information at Austin.

Loriene's accomplishments span decades, and it is her hope that her legacy will be carried on by the students she has taught, spreading the love of reading among Native American children while honoring and preserving their own heritage and wisdom. When Loriene received the 2020 Provost's Distinguished Service Academy award at the University of Texas at Austin, dean Eric T. Meyer summed up her work: "I am absolutely delighted that Professor Roy's dedication and service to the iSchool, to the university, and beyond have been recognized by her being selected as one of the inaugural members awarded this honor. She has such a strong dedication to mentoring and inclusion, and this not only rewards such dedication but also allows her to use it as a platform to help others follow in her footsteps."

Loriene Roy's time has come. Her *mana* (derived from Hawaiian and Maori cultures, meaning "spiritual energy and influence") is strong, and the impact of her work will be felt for years to come.

AWARDS AND HONORS

- Provost's Distinguished Service Academy, The University of Texas at Austin, 2020–2025
- Emerald Literati Award for Excellence, 2018

- Distinguished Service Award, American Indian Library Association, 2015
- Distinguished Alumnus Award, Graduate School of Library and Information Science, University of Illinois at Urbana-Champaign, 2014
- Sarah Vann Award, ALA Hawai'i Student Chapter, University of Hawai'i Manoa Library and Information Science Program, 2014
- Leadership Award, National Conference of Tribal Archives, Libraries, and Museums, 2009
- APEX Award for Publication Excellence, We Shall Remain, Library Event Kit, 2009
- State of Texas, Senate Proclamation No. 127, for dedication to profession, July 2007
- Honor Dance, National Museum of the American Indian, Washington, DC, June 22, 2007
- Equality Award, American Library Association, 2006
- Mover and Shaker, *Library Journal*, 2005
- Outstanding Alumna, School of Information Resources and Library Science, University of Arizona, 2002
- Joe and Bettie Branson Ward Excellence Award for Research, Teaching, or Demonstration Activities that Contribute to Changes of Positive Value to Society, University of Texas at Austin, 2001
- James W. Vick Texas Excellence Award for Academic Advisors, GSLIS, University of Texas at Austin, 1992

Sharice Lynnette Davids

HO-CHUNK NATION

Ad astra per aspera (a Latin phrase meaning "to the stars through difficulties").

THE STATE MOTTO OF KANSAS

Ad astra per aspera" were the final words of the victory speech delivered by Sharice Lynnette Davids, an enrolled member of Ho-Chunk Nation of Wisconsin, when she was elected in 2018 to the US House of Representatives for the state of Kansas. Sharice broke all the barriers by being one of only two Native American women ever elected to the US House of Representatives as well as being a member of the LGBTQ (lesbian, gay, bisexual, transgender, queer) community and the first person in her family to earn a college degree.

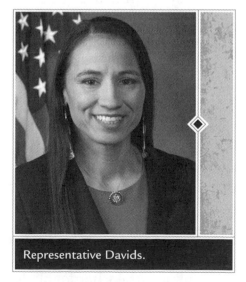

Representative Davids.

Sharice's story is one of hard work and opportunity that she says she owes to her mother's support, a good public education system, and prospects that she recognized and took advantage of. "I went from Johnson County Community College to Cornell Law School and then on to the Obama White House—all opportunities that stem from my access to quality public education," she said.

Recognizing possibilities in life and grasping chances as they arise seems to be a common thread in the Davids family. Sharice's grandfather, Fred Davids, was born in 1927 into the Stockbridge-Munsee Band of Mohicans in Oneida, Wisconsin. He enlisted in the US Army at the age of eighteen. His career spanned almost thirty years and three major conflicts, including World War II, the Korean War, and the Vietnam conflict. His daughter, Crystal Herriage, followed in his footsteps and is an Army veteran as well.

Crystal served in the US Army as a drill sergeant and gave birth to Sharice Davids in Frankfurt, Germany, on May 22, 1980. She raised Sharice and her two younger brothers on her own as a single mother. The family moved to many military bases around the world throughout Sharice's childhood. After serving in the military for more than twenty years, Crystal retired from the Army and moved her family back to Kansas, where she worked for the US Postal Service.

Growing up in an environment of constant change inspired Sharice to become a strong and independent woman. Sharice says she felt accepted by her Kansas community when she was growing up, although she credits her mother for much of the respect and support she received. Her mother encouraged her to "just be me," Sharice says. This advice prompted her decision to come out as a teenager. When she started dating another girl in high school, her mother accepted it without any questions or concerns.

As a youngster, Sharice developed a strong admiration for Bruce Lee and his martial arts skills, work ethic, and discipline. When her family lived in Germany, she had taken tae kwon do classes, but when they moved back to the US, training was too costly for her single mom to afford. "There were three of us, and it was just too expensive to pay for me to do martial arts practice," Sharice recalls. It wasn't until she was a nineteen-year-old college student that Sharice became involved in martial arts again, taking classes in karate, capoeira, and then combative tae kwon do a few years later.

Education has been a priority for Sharice Davids throughout her life. She worked hard and sacrificed much in order to attain her law degree (juris doctor) from Cornell University. It wasn't easy being raised by a single mother, being first in her family to attend college, and having to work while in school. She did stints as a carhop at a Sonic drive-in and as a bartender at a Marriott hotel, among other jobs. The determination to learn and grow inspired her success.

While working on her bachelor's degree at the University of Missouri–Kansas City, Sharice learned a valuable lesson in time management that has continued to serve her well. She worked her way through school, carrying a heavy class load, with leadership courses being her favorites. All the while, Sharice honed her skills as an amateur martial arts competitor. Although Sharice was a formidable opponent in the mixed martial arts ring, she knew better than to try to make a career out of the sport she had grown to love. She made the decision instead to focus on her law school studies.

After graduating from Cornell Law School in 2010, Sharice returned home to the Kansas City area and worked at SNR Denton (now Dentons), one of the world's largest law firms. Her area of specialty was mergers and acquisitions. As the years passed, Sharice felt an urge to turn her attention back to Indian Country. In 2012, she left her lucrative law practice at a prestigious firm to work with tribes to promote economic development in Native communities. She headed to the tribal lands in South Dakota.

Sharice worked on the Pine Ridge Indian Reservation, home of the Oglala Lakota and one of the poorest regions in the

Sharice and her mom at graduation, Cornell University, Cornell Law School.

country. While living on the Pine Ridge Indian Reservation, Sharice saw the inequities and blatant discrimination the tribes there experienced. When she moved to South Dakota, Sharice was told that lodging would be available for staff because of the sparse availability of housing on the reservation. But later Sharice learned that she wasn't eligible. "I wasn't able to get housing with my partner because we were in a same-sex relationship," she says. Her relationship violated the housing policies. This reminded her, once again, that laws and policies are not always applied equally, despite it being fifty years since the 1968 Fair Housing Act became law.

Her time on the reservation included work as the director of economic development at the Red Cloud Indian School and, later, as deputy director of the Thunder Valley Community Development Corporation. She launched an after-school program to encourage high school students to pursue entrepreneurial ventures and supported alumni and community members through the creation of a small-business assistance program. A colleague shared that her leadership as an Indigenous woman was always a source of inspiration for the young people she worked with.

Sharice's entrepreneurial spirit spurred her to start her own business in 2013. She opened a coffee shop in Rapid City, South Dakota, called Hoka Coffee. The goal was to create jobs in the area and buy ingredients from local Indigenous farms. Unfortunately, due to limited funding, Sharice had to make the difficult decision to close the company.

By 2016, Sharice had worked on the Pine Ridge Indian Reservation for five years and had witnessed the barriers and inequities against Native people that stemmed from state and federal policies. She decided to apply to become a White House fellow, a position in a highly competitive leadership and public service program. She was one of sixteen people selected to participate in the program and was placed with the US Department of Housing and Urban Development during the last year of President Obama's administration. Because of her experience on the reservation and her time in Washington, DC, Sharice's political aspirations were beginning to take shape.

In the months before the 2018 midterm elections, Sharice observed the frustration that had been growing in Kansas's Third Congressional District. She saw an opportunity to unseat the person who had held the position since 2011. Originally, it was hoped that a Democratic opponent would step up. Sharice sought to recruit other female candidates whom she thought had a fighting chance to defeat the incumbent, but that plan hit a major obstacle. No one would agree to run for the office.

Frustrated by the lack of interest, Sharice and her colleagues sat around her kitchen table one evening to try to come up with another plan. "We had talked to probably six different people and were getting nowhere," she says. Although Sharice didn't set out to be a trailblazer, she decided that if she was that committed to change, she would run for the office herself. So began the history-making campaign. On November 6, 2018, Sharice Davids won the hard-fought election. Finally, Native American women had a seat at the table.

From the moment she made the decision to run for Congress, Sharice has stayed true to her campaign promises. She has been a tireless champion for bills that support construction and building funds, transparency in drug costs, insurance accountability, women's business centers, and others. She has personally experienced the crushing impact that college student loans can have on graduates as they try to move into the workforce. She is a strong advocate of policies that enable people to refinance student loans at lower rates and make it easier to renegotiate loan terms.

Another piece of legislation that Sharice actively supported was the Paycheck Fairness Act of 2019. The bill, which was first introduced to Congress in 1997 by Representative Rosa DeLauro, ensured that men and women would receive equal pay for equal work. In March 2019, the act was approved by the House of Representatives but failed in the Senate.

Sharice Davids has made her mark in Congress as a strong and thoughtful member who is in it for the long haul. This was valiantly demonstrated when the members of the House of Representatives had to make the difficult vote on the impeachment of President Donald Trump in 2019. Around 7:00 p.m. on September 25, Representative Davids announced that she would support the impeachment inquiry. Sharice was the 218th member of Congress to announce her support. This was a significant number because 218 votes is a majority in the House. Any article of impeachment that receives that many votes will be sent to the Senate for trial. Sharice bravely cast that vote, which determined the fate of the president of the United States.

"She's not a show-off," Representative Cheri Bustos said about her colleague. "She's an athlete, and if you've ever known any high-level athletes, you know that they're disciplined and methodical and nail all the fundamentals." With regard to the respect she has received from her congressional colleagues,

Sharice says, "You have to build relationships and learn what is of interest to other members of Congress and what they've taken a lead on for a long time. Then you can discover where there's space for you to contribute to the conversation." This approach has helped her build clout with party leaders, who see her as a rising star.

Sharice Davids and Deb Haaland (see page 59) are the first two Native American women to serve in Congress. Sharice said she can't imagine having this experience without Representative Haaland. The pair shared an emotional embrace on the House floor on the first day of the 116th session of Congress. Both were part of a record number of ninety-eight women who were elected to the House of Representatives in 2018. Sharice's win changed a district that hadn't elected a Democrat to Congress in a decade.

Sharice's commitment to diversity, equity, and understanding is demonstrated in her outreach to young people. During her visit to Q Space Chat, an LGBTQ youth group, she talked about coming out to her family, listened to their stories about bullying, and offered words of comfort. "She took time to hug each and every one of them and take a picture with them," said Q Space Chat's founder and executive director Cassandra Peters. "It was just so comforting for them to think that this person is a politician and cares about them."

On her view of the future, Sharice says, "It's rare to step back and realize that we were in the middle of a revolution. Whenever legislation is passed, we need to think about how it affects all varieties of communities." She feels that if more

Representative Davids with Representative Deb Haaland.

The swearing in of Representative Sharice Davids, US House of Representatives.

people with diverse experiences can be included in the conversation, it will be easier to identify those who have been left out and need their voices to be heard. Diversity in ideas and cultures enrich the decision-making process and promote acceptance and understanding. This is the standard Sharice Davids believes in and lives by.

AWARDS AND HONORS

- Spirit of Enterprise Award, US Chamber of Commerce, 2020
- Pride50 award, NBC News, 2019
- Cofounder and host of *Starty Pants*, a podcast highlighting and celebrating people with unique paths, interesting business ideas, and niche markets, with a focus on featuring guests who are women, people of color, and LGBTQ community members, 2017–2018
- Member of the founding board of directors and initial chairperson of the board, Twelve Clans, Inc., Ho-Chunk Nation, 2015–2016

Roberta Jamieson

KANYEN'KEHÀ:KA, SIX NATIONS OF THE GRAND RIVER TERRITORY

Being a change-maker requires opportunity. Sometimes you need to create it, but other times you just need to see it and get hold of it. Timing is everything.

ROBERTA JAMIESON

oberta Jamieson has lived a life of "firsts"—opportunities that she recognized and grabbed hold of. It's rare to find a person who has accomplished as much as Roberta and who has had such a positive influence on youth. Because of Roberta's deep belief in Native youth, thousands of young people have received an education and given back to their communities for the greater good.

Roberta was born in 1953 on Six Nations of the Grand River Territory reserve near Brantford, Ontario, Canada. Her father, Robert Jamieson, was of Kanyen'kehà:ka (Mohawk) heritage, and her mother was second-generation Irish from the Ottawa Valley. Robert was a talented musician and toured with the United Service Organizations, entertaining troops during World War II. After the war, he returned to the Six Nations, where he met Phyllis McCann, a young Irish woman who was working as a nurse on the reserve. They were married and settled down to raise a large, close-knit family with eight children.

To support their family, Roberta's parents ran a restaurant on the Six Nations reserve called Bobby's Diner, where the children worked alongside their parents, learning the importance of hard work and a good education. At twelve years old, Roberta was waiting tables. That was when she first observed the unfair treatment and negative attitudes toward Indigenous people. While she was serving a meal to the Six Nations chief and a government Indian agent, the inequality facing her people became apparent. The conversation between the chief and the government agent made it clear that the agent was not going to allow anything to be done without his approval. The ideas and suggestions proposed by the chief were ignored unless the agent found them agreeable. Roberta says, "I found it abhorrent. It motivated me to change our circumstances." She recognized that change could only come through education—both formal education and the ability to listen and observe, to learn from the elders and those around her.

The Six Nations Grand River Territory is the largest of the First Nations reserves. It is where Roberta grew up and received her elementary and secondary education. The teachers were Native and non-Native, and they followed a government-approved curriculum that taught things that were contrary to what the students knew to be true. For instance, they knew Columbus did not discover America. That truth had been passed down through the years from generation to generation, elders to parents to children. The Indigenous people have lived in the Americas since time immemorial, before written record, oral history, or even memory. These types of inconsistencies spawned mistrust in the minds of the students.

Roberta saw many of her classmates dropping out of school. She says, "We sat in a classroom learning from a book about people we could not remotely relate to and who don't reflect our community. When you don't have your identity validated, it's easy to check out." This unfortunate reality

Roberta Jamieson.

stayed with Roberta. It shaped her life and formed her commitment to address the disconnect that Indigenous young people have to formal education.

Roberta was fortunate to have a teacher who had stepped away from the mandated curriculum and impressed on her students that they needed to look behind what they were being told. She said that it was healthy to question what they were being taught and that the students must take into account their identity and their history. This sage advice helped Roberta to become more confident in her identity. She recognizes that people need room to be themselves and the space to be different. Today, she tells the youth she works with that all people are unique and that it's good to acknowledge and respect our differences.

In 1970, Roberta enrolled at McGill University, intending to study medicine. She had a great-uncle who was a doctor, and she was determined that she would follow in his footsteps. But while she was delving into her premed studies, she became entangled in a conflict involving the James Bay Project, which aimed to construct a series of hydroelectric power stations on the La Grande River in northwestern Quebec, Canada. As part of this massive project, the James Bay Cree's traditional hunting and fishing grounds were to be flooded. As a student, Roberta advocated for and defended the tribe's rights. She even debated with Canada's minister of Indian Affairs about the land-claim issues related to building the dam. She realized that the best way to help First Nations people defend their rights and interests was to learn the law. "Our people need legal skills if we're going to secure our proper place in Canada," Roberta says.

This political awakening and desire to defend First Nations rights led Roberta to change her studies from premed to law. She received her bachelor of laws (LLB) degree in 1976 from the University of Western Ontario, making her the first Indigenous woman in Canada to graduate from law school.

After graduation, Roberta became part of the Canadian Indian Rights Commission secretariat. From 1978 to 1982, she worked at the Indian Commission of Ontario as the executive assistant to the commissioner, senior policy adviser, and senior mediator. Roberta had experienced firsthand how Indigenous people were not respected, and she was intent on changing that.

In the book *Great Women Leaders*, author Heather Ball describes how, as a youngster, Roberta learned about Mohawk political traditions. The process of "holding council"—a time when people gather, trade opinions, and keep talking until consensus is reached—is the tradition that Roberta has honored over the years. Ball states, "It was clear from the work

Roberta had done negotiating for the rights of First Nations people that she had found her calling. She continued the tradition of holding council, believing decisions should be reached by discussion and consultation in a coolheaded manner, rather than through angry confrontation. This is Roberta's signature style and one of the reasons she is such a trusted negotiator."

In 2001, Roberta became the first woman elected as chief of the Six Nations. The election marked a significant change in leadership on the reserve. With 75 percent of the council members newly elected, Roberta sought to create a more inclusive system of decision making, a conflict-resolution process, and a separation between Six Nations politics and its administration.

This period of time for Roberta revealed the difficulties often faced by people in leadership roles. She faced challenges that demanded difficult decisions. But she drew on her exceptional skills in diplomacy and persevered in addressing the needs of the Six Nations people. Roberta served her elected term as chief and then considered her next options. She stated, "Three years ago there were serious challenges in this community. People were concerned about the lack of accountability and transparency at the council level. . . . A lot of people asked me if I would step forward, given my background in law and as an ombudsman, to put my name forward and stand for election as chief. . . . I decided it was my responsibility to step forward and work with the community in addressing these problems and getting us on the right track, and I think I've done my job." She did not run for a second term. It was time for her to move on to what would become her life's work.

Roberta was about to make a life-altering choice that focused her energy on what she's always believed: education is the tool that will change lives and change the environment for Indigenous people. In October 2004, Roberta ended her term as chief at Six Nations, and on November 4, she assumed leader-

Roberta with Indspire students.

ship of the National Aboriginal Achievement Foundation (now Indspire). This nonprofit organization encourages and empowers young Indigenous people to advance their educational and career aspirations. Under Roberta's leadership, Indspire has provided mentorships, bursaries (aid based on a student's financial need), and scholarships to ensure that more youth on reserves will graduate high school. The organization also helps educators, both Indigenous and non-Indigenous, provide positive reinforcement of students' Indigenous identities and ways of learning to strengthen their sense of being part of a larger community.

The Indspire organization is a crucial element in bettering the lives of students in Canada. Funds raised from government, corporate, and private sectors have provided annual disbursements to support Indigenous students in education beyond high school. These awards have provided more than $100 million in financial support to more than thirty-five thousand students. On average, 90 percent of students who have received funding have graduated from a postsecondary institution. "We need to bust the myths and stereotypes about our people that continue to abound," Roberta says. Indspire's purpose is to see that, within a generation, every Indigenous student will graduate.

Since her formative years at McGill University, Roberta Jamieson has been an extraordinary advocate for Indigenous people. She has always believed that Indigenous knowledge is a rich cultural and human resource that provides the chance to embrace history while building the future.

Thousands of youth have benefited from Roberta's dedication and work, but, as the saying goes, the only constant is change. Roberta plans to retire in 2021, when she steps down from her position at Indspire. Her new role of being a *dudah* (grandmother) for her three grandchildren will undoubtedly bring new challenges and joys for Roberta and her husband, Tom Hill. Roberta's influence will be remembered in the beliefs that have always been her driving force: "Understand that, as a citizen, you not only have rights but also responsibilities. Responsibility means to use your talents and resources to give back to your community." Ever humble, Roberta believes that every person can be a role model and has the potential to inspire others.

AWARDS AND HONORS

- Indigenous Women in Leadership Award, Canadian Council for Aboriginal Business, 2018
- Inter-American Award, Conference of the Americas on International Education, 2017
- Canada's Most Powerful Women: Top 100 Award, Women's Executive Network, 2009, 2010, 2016
- Women of Distinction Award, YWCA, 2016
- Officer of the Order of Canada, 2016

- David C. Smith Award, Council of Ontario Universities, 2014
- Indigenous Peoples Council Award, Indigenous Bar Association, 2001, 2012
- Queen Elizabeth II Diamond Jubilee Medal, 2012
- Deo Kernahan Memorial Award, Urban Alliance on Race Relations in Toronto, 2002
- Harmony Award, Harmony Movement, 2002
- National Aboriginal Achievement Award for Law and Justice, 1998
- Golden Eagle Feather Award, National Association of Friendship Centres, 1997
- Member of the Order of Canada, 1994
- Mary Parker Follett Award, International Society of Professionals in Dispute Resolution, 1992
- Goodman Fellow, Faculty of Law, University of Toronto, 1991
- Keepers of Our Culture Award, First Nations Women in Canada, 1984
- Outstanding Contribution Award, National Indian Brotherhood, 1977
- Honorary degrees from twenty-six institutions of higher education

Deb Haaland

PUEBLO OF LAGUNA

As a kid, I never could have imagined today. I will leave the ladder down behind me so girls of color know they can be anything they want to be.

DEB HAALAND, ON HER ELECTION TO
THE US HOUSE OF REPRESENTATIVES

rowing up an "army brat" was not easy for Debra Ann (Deb) Haaland and her three siblings. A military family, the Haalands were often moving from one military base to another around the country. Deb attended thirteen schools before her family finally settled down in Albuquerque, New Mexico, where she finished high school.

Deb's parents, Major J. D. "Dutch" Haaland and Mary Toya, were both veterans of the United States military. Her father retired from the US Marine Corps after serving for thirty years and was a decorated officer. He was the recipient of fifteen medals during his career, including two Purple Hearts and the Silver Star for conspicuous gallantry for his actions in the Vietnam War. Haaland's mother served in the US Navy when the couple was stationed in California.

Mary Toya is Laguna, and Deb's father, who died in 2005, was Norwegian American. Deb was born December 2, 1960,

Representative Deb Haaland.

in Winslow, Arizona. She is a thirty-fifth-generation New Mexican who is an enrolled member of the Pueblo of Laguna. She also has Jemez Pueblo heritage. Deb's family was raised in a Pueblo household. She says, "In spite of the fact that we moved around a lot, we still kept those strong ties to my grandparents and our community of Laguna Pueblo. You can be Native wherever you are."

The Haaland children always considered their maternal grandparents' place on the Laguna Pueblo as their home base. The house had no running water, and when she was young, Deb would be sent down to the spigot in the middle of the village to fill two buckets to the brim. She'd carry the full buckets three blocks back to her grandmother's one-room house so she and her siblings could drink or have a bath. The house also didn't have electricity, but that didn't stop Deb's grandmother from teaching her how to bake in their brick-and-clay oven. In addition, Deb's grandfather taught her about gardening, which she learned by working beside him in the fields and picking worms off the ears of corn.

Deb's ancestors have lived in this rural New Mexico village for nearly one thousand years. Although her grandparents are gone, Deb's grandmother's house is still standing—and so is the spigot. Deb says, "I think that's where I learned to be very conservative with water. When you have to haul your own, you conserve."

With regard to her ethnicity, Deb states, "I am who I am. I choose to identify as Native American. That's who I am. That's the culture I'm closest to because my mom and my grandmother taught me so much."

Deb believes that the intergenerational power of women and unbreakable family ties are embedded in her DNA. She and her two sisters and brother were raised by their mother while their father was often away from home on service deployments. Deb views this maternal strength as one of the many sacrifices mothers make to keep their families together.

Family is sacred in Native American culture, and love and respect are taught from a young age. Mary Toya showed her children the importance of family and responsibility through the attention and care she gave them. Because her husband was frequently gone, Deb's mother would make her children write letters to their dad every night at the kitchen table. She realized there was always a chance that their father could be injured or, worse yet, killed in action, and she wanted to be sure that he knew how much his children loved him. Dutch died in 2005, many years after he retired. The family opened his military footlocker after his death and found all those letters bound with string and stashed away for safekeeping.

Mary Toya did not work outside the home until Deb turned fourteen. "Up to that point," Deb says, "my mom made us study hard after school each day and appreciate what my dad called 'a free education.'" Deb graduated from Highland High School in Albuquerque, where her teachers inspired her to want to learn more.

After high school, Deb continued working at the bakery where she had been employed since she was fifteen years old. Her job was helping customers and decorating cakes. Although she enjoyed school and loved to learn, Deb did not go on to college. Neither of her parents went to college, and, like so many young people at that age, she didn't know what she needed to do to get there or whom to ask for help. She didn't know that it had been her high school guidance counselor's role to help her find her way to college.

One day, at the age of twenty-eight, when she was braiding her hair and getting ready for work, Deb had a moment of clarity. She asked herself, "Am I going to be doing this for the rest of my life?" The answer was a resounding no! A family friend at the Bureau of Indian Affairs helped her apply to the University of New Mexico, and then Deb Haaland was on her way to a life she never could have imagined.

Deb knew that getting a college degree was the right path for her. Still, it wasn't easy taking classes and working to pay her way through school. She was in her senior year when she found out she was pregnant, but she kept moving forward with her studies. Months later, she proudly marched in her graduation ceremony, receiving her bachelor's degree in English in 1994. Four days later, she gave birth to her daughter, Somáh.

After completing her bachelor's degree, Deb's innovative spirit led her to start a small business. Food is an important element in Native American culture. Powwows, celebrations, and family gatherings all center on shared meals. Deb comes from a long line of good cooks, so food is what she decided to focus her business on. She started a salsa company called

The swearing in of Representative Deb Haaland, US House of Representatives.

Pueblo Salsa and traveled around the Southwest selling her product at a variety of events. As a single mother, Deb took Somáh everywhere with her, forging a mother-daughter relationship based on trust and love. With Alanis Morissette's *Jagged Little Pill* blasting from the car stereo, they sold her product. "I wanted Somáh with me twenty-four hours a day because I felt like I needed to influence her at that early age, and it paid off," Deb says.

For several years, Deb ran Pueblo Salsa, doing all the production and canning on her own. In time, she became the first chairwoman elected to the Laguna Development Corporation's board of directors, overseeing business operations of the second largest tribal gaming enterprise in New Mexico. Deb successfully advocated for the Laguna Development Corporation to create policies and commitments to earth-friendly business practices. She is also a former tribal administrator and has managed a local service provider for adults with developmental disabilities. All of these positions demonstrated Deb's concern and commitment to her Native people and strengthened her desire to encourage positive change.

As the years went by, many opportunities were presented to her. In 2003, Deb decided to return to the University of New Mexico to earn a degree in law. One day, while she was in law school, a classmate flipped open his laptop to reveal a red, white, and blue John Kerry bumper sticker. (John Kerry was the Democratic Party's presidential nominee in 2004.) Deb asked her classmate how she could get involved. That question led to years of volunteering for various political candidates and causes.

A couple of years later, her former constitutional law professor was recruiting participants for a women's candidate training program called Emerge New Mexico. She asked Deb to apply. Deb had never thought of running for office but had trust in her professor's judgment and decided to go for it.

Deb graduated from the program in 2007 and soon volunteered to work on Barack Obama's presidential campaign. She ferried carloads of people out to the pueblos to canvass and eventually became Obama's Native American vote director for New Mexico. Deb ran for lieutenant governor two years later (her mom became a Democrat so she could vote for her in the primary), and although she lost the general election, she later became chair of the state Democratic Party in 2015.

Deb Haaland traveled down many roads while determining how she could be a strong advocate for Native people and the population at large. As her political vision started to take shape, she knew she could identify with people who deserved a place at the table. She knew what it was like to be poor. She says, "Some of the experiences I had as a single parent—being on food stamps, piecing together health care for my daughter—helped me to understand what 99 percent of my district experiences. I felt I could be an authentic voice and represent them because I had been through what they were going through."

Her drive to connect, understand, and support others led Deb to an event that left a permanent imprint on her. When she was chair of the Democratic Party in New Mexico, she heard about the Standing Rock Sioux tribe in North Dakota, which was protesting the construction of the Dakota Access Pipeline. This pipeline would carry more than five hundred thousand barrels of crude oil a day to Illinois. The Sioux feared the pipeline would threaten the reservation's water supply, should it ever break. Deb stuffed a suitcase full of green chiles and got on a plane to join the protest.

She spent four days in the Oceti Sakowin camp. She called tribal leaders to rally support for the cause. She talked with the people at the camp who had traveled across the country to stand up for Native American rights. One night, she opened her suitcase stash and cooked a big pot of green-chile stew over the fire, along with homemade tortillas, so the protesters could taste a traditional Pueblo meal. Jodi Archambault Gillette remembers that night well: "As Indigenous women, we have responsibilities that are sacred to us. She gave us her traditional food. That was beautiful."

Time spent with the Standing Rock Sioux created memories that will stay with Deb forever. "It was a wonderful place," she says, recalling the camp where protesters stayed for months. "They had singing and dancing at nighttime. It was really remarkable that they were protesting in such a strong cultural and peaceful way." Deb's advocacy for justice has been her rallying cry throughout her adult life and is what led to her seat in Congress.

While Deb was taking classes in 2000 at the University of California, Los Angeles (UCLA), she and Somáh were living in a one-bedroom apartment in Santa Monica, California, and Somáh was in first grade. Somáh was taking after-school drama lessons at the Santa Monica Playhouse when the theater lost its funding. Deb launched a campaign to save the

Deb with her daughter, Somáh.

playhouse, canvassing the community with six-year-old Somáh in tow. Mother and daughter prevailed, and the playhouse still operates today. Somáh went on to major in theater at the University of New Mexico.

Deb is always the advocate, and her empathy and motivation spurred her historic win for her seat in the 116th US Congress, House of Representatives. Together with Representative Sharice Davids (see page 43) from Kansas, Deb entered the House floor; they were the first Native American women to ever hold seats in that chamber. In doing so, Deb's fight for better funding for education for Native children and adults, improvements on tribal lands, and addressing the horrific problem of missing and murdered Indigenous people continued.

Deb supported the Justice for Native Women Survivors of Sexual Violence Act, which increases efforts in confronting the crisis of murdered and missing Indigenous women. Reports have shown at least four out of five American Indian and Alaskan Native women and girls have experienced some form of violence in their lives. The Justice for Native Survivors of Sexual Violence Act restores criminal jurisdiction to tribal courts so they can prosecute cases of sexual assault, sex trafficking, and stalking crimes in Indian Country.

Deb Haaland has worn many hats throughout her life: single mother struggling to provide for her daughter, small-business owner, political activist, and a member of Congress. She has experienced many "firsts" in her life, including being the first Native American woman to sit in the Speaker's chair and preside over a House of Representatives floor debate on the For the People Act of 2019, transformative legislation that seeks to end corruption in politics and ensure fair access to the ballot box.

During her first two years in Congress, Deb Haaland's reputation as a strong leader, pragmatist, and problem-solver has led to yet another "first." Deb's Native upbringing, broad experience, and staunch defense of federal and tribal lands garnered recognition by 2020 President-elect Joe Biden, resulting in her nomination to lead the US Department of the Interior. With congressional approval, Deb would be the first Native American to hold a cabinet secretary position. While discussing her nomination, Deb reflected back on her early life, stating, "Growing up in my mother's Pueblo household made me fierce." She vowed that same ongoing commitment with this new opportunity.

Deb offers this advice for young people: "Whatever career path is taken, there will be obstacles, but they don't have to get in the way. If you are passionate enough [about helping your community], you can move forward, jump over the obstacles, or go around them. . . . Never forget where you came from. Every day when I wake up and say my morning prayers, I thank our Creator for giving me the family I have."

On the morning Deb was to be sworn in to Congress, her office was buzzing with many folks in bolo ties, cowboy boots, and ribbon dresses. Friends and family from New Mexico were there to share this historic moment. The room quieted as Deb's eighty-three-year-old mother was wheeled in. Deb steered her mother into her office and pointed to the few pieces of decor she had on her shelves: framed black-and-white photos of her parents and grandparents and a kachina doll from her mother.

Mary Toya reached for her daughter's hand as she surveyed the wall and tears welled in her eyes. "I'm so proud of you," she said.

Since that historic day in January 2018, when Debra Ann Haaland was sworn into the US House of Representatives, her life has continued on a trajectory that no one in that room could have imagined. On March 15, 2021, Representative Haaland was sworn in as the Secretary of the Interior, making her the first Native American to hold a cabinet position. That night, Deb's image was projected on the side of the Interior building in Washington, DC, along with with this text: "Our Ancestors' Dreams Come True."

AWARDS AND HONORS

- Outstanding New Member Award, Friends of the National Services, 2020
- Speaker's chair, first Native American woman to preside over debate in US House of Representatives, 2019
- Woman Warrior Award, Native Americans in Philanthropy, 2019
- Vanguard Award, National Center for Lesbian Rights, 2019
- William C. Velasquez Trailblazer Award, US Hispanic Leadership Institute's National Conference, 2019
- Board of directors, Laguna Development Corporation, 2010–2015
- Delegate, Democratic National Convention, 2008

Elsie Marie Knott

MISSISSAUGA OJIBWE

She had enough spunk to get out there, and she was right for the job. . . . She opened our eyes.

NORMAN KNOTT

As the old baby-blue hearse bumped and rumbled down the gravel highway to Lakefield, sixteen miles away, its passengers were not headed for the hereafter. They were very much alive and well. Those on board were five motivated teenagers aspiring to do what most of their friends could not—attend high school and get a high school diploma. Elsie Marie Knott was the driver of the old jalopy and was determined that those students would have the same opportunity to attend high school as white students did.

Elsie was a force of nature who found it nearly impossible to take no for an answer. She

Elsie with photo from her early years.

was born of humble beginnings and experienced abject poverty, but nothing stopped her unflappable determination to make life better for her family and her tribal band. She accomplished much in her life, most notably becoming the first Indigenous woman elected chief of a First Nations tribe in Canada.

Elsie Marie Taylor was born on September 20, 1922, to Esther Mae and George Henry Taylor into the Mississauga Mud Lake band. She was the fourth of seven children, including Hollis, Perry, Donald, Rolland, Joyce, and Stella. The Taylors were a well-established family in the Mud Lake reserve community. Both parents had been born on the reserve and had enjoyed the benefits of a large traditional extended family. Elsie grew up on the reserve surrounded by her maternal and paternal grandparents and many aunts, uncles, and cousins.

Elsie's father worked as the caretaker of the band's office. He attended band and community meetings held at the office and then stayed to clean up afterward. Elsie would often go with her father to these events. Later, they would discuss topics that came up at the meeting and question why certain decisions were made. Even as a child, Elsie was curious about politics, community issues, and social matters. She wanted to understand the functions of the community and how it worked.

Elsie's childhood was spent in isolation from the outside world, and she spoke only the Ojibwe language until she entered school at nine years old. She started late due to an illness that prevented her from walking. After recovering, she joined the other reserve children at the local school run by the Department of Indian Affairs. Much like the government-run schools in the US, the goal was to force Native children to "fit in" with white society by doing away with their culture and language. Native children were expected to discard their Indian identity and culture and were forced to speak only English. At the reserve school, anyone caught talking their

Indian language had their name written on the blackboard with a big capital *X* beside it to shame the student.

Elsie completed her studies up to grade eight, but with no high school on the reserve, her formal education ended. Once she was finished with school, she was considered an adult and ready for marriage. Elsie said, "Nobody ever talked to me about a career. Women just got married." When she was fifteen years old, her parents arranged for her to marry Cecil Knott, a man twelve years her elder.

By the time she was twenty, Elsie had three children—Edward, Glenn, and Rita—and was struggling with her home life. Unfortunately, Cecil was plagued with tuberculosis, a disease that prevented him from holding a steady job, and the family was reliant on social assistance (welfare). The twelve dollars a month they received was crucial for the Knott family to afford food and shelter, but it was a difficult time. Cecil eventually died of a stroke in 1962, leaving Elsie a widow at thirty-nine years old, and she never remarried.

Elsie considered the dire straits the family was in and concluded that she had no option but to look for work. She was not above doing menial labor to support her family. She dug worms and caught minnows to sell to fishermen for bait and picked berries in a town past Toronto, more than one hundred miles away. Unfortunately, after picking for five weeks, she barely made enough money to get back home! Elsie was not particular about her jobs, as long as she got paid. She worked hard as a chambermaid at the hotel in Lakefield, sewed pajamas for Indian children in federal hospitals (earning thirty-five cents a pair), and sewed quilts to sell to tourists. One of the jobs she held for seventeen years was working as a housekeeper for a wealthy New Jersey family who vacationed in the Curve Lake area. It was said they were perhaps the only family in Canada to have an Indian chief washing their dishes and making their beds.

Elsie's stalwart determination to provide for her family meant that she sought out every opportunity to make money.

Elsie at story time.

It happened that the lack of a high school on the reserve turned out to be the very thing that moved Elsie Knott ahead. Five children from the Mud Lake reserve wanted to continue their education beyond grade eight. The Indian agent hired a local man for fifteen dollars a week to drive the students to and from the main highway, where they were picked up by the county school bus. One day, the man failed to pick up the children after school, and they had to walk the five miles home. Needless to say, this resulted in upset children, angry parents, and an Indian agent who needed to find a more reliable driver. Knowing Elsie's financial situation, the Indian agent presented an opportunity to her for employment. He approached Elsie about driving the children, just until he could find someone else. Thus began her thirty-one years as a school bus driver.

At first, Elsie drove the students in her own car, an old green Ford Model A. The number of passengers soon outgrew her Ford, so she convinced the reserve's Indian agent to cosign a bank loan with her to purchase a used hearse for two hundred dollars. She installed bench seats on the floor of the old vehicle to accommodate the growing number of students. Every day, the young mother would pick up the students at the end of their lane and drive them to high school, come rain, shine, or ice and snow. Eventually, even the converted hearse became too small for the daily transport of children. Elsie saw an opportunity and took it. Over the years she purchased two seventy-eight-passenger school buses and established Knott's Bus Service.

Since the reserve was so isolated, most of the children were not exposed to non-Native people on a regular basis. Attending school off the reserve was a challenge. They were discriminated against and often called racial slurs, and their school bus was regularly pelted with rocks. Despite the difficulties that confronted Elsie and the students, Elsie valued education and encouraged the reserve's children to get a high school degree and more. She wanted reserve children to succeed in life and helped them in every way possible. Referring to Elsie's strong leadership, artist Randy Knott said, "I was so scared to leave the reserve and go to the other school. But through her we all got brave." Another student, Winston Taylor, recalls, "Her example inspired me when I went back to school. She was that kind of lady who made up her mind to do something, and she just did it." Elsie continued to drive the children for more than thirty years, until two years before her death, when she had to give up the wheel due to chronic knee problems.

Although Elsie saw herself as a shy person lacking in confidence, she became stronger out of necessity and shared that confidence with others. She was creative, had good business sense, and was always tuned in to the needs of the people around her. These were traits that benefited her throughout her life, especially with the challenges she would face in the years to come.

In 1951, Canada was experiencing many changes in how the federal and provincial (provinces are similar to states in the United States) governments worked with the First Nations tribes. The Indian Act, established in 1876, allowed for the Canadian government to control nearly all aspects of Indigenous culture. The policy stated that Native people could not leave the reserve without a pass from the Indian agent. Partly, this rationale was developed to prevent Native people from traveling to distant residential schools to see their children. The Indian Act was especially denigrating toward Indigenous women, because it took away their rights and freedom. In September 1951, the Indian Act was amended to allow Indigenous women to vote and be elected to positions in band governments. This was a game changer for Elsie Marie Knott and other women who would follow in her footsteps.

Elsie was well known and respected on her reserve. She was seen as a hard worker who involved herself in the community doing everything from driving the school bus to playing on the women's softball team, all while supporting and raising a family. It's no wonder that community members asked her to run for chief of the Curve Lake First Nation. This was only three years after changes to the Indian Act allowed Indigenous women to vote and run for office in their bands. Elsie was skeptical but allowed her name to be put on the ballot. No one was more surprised than she when the results were announced and she won the election by a landslide. In 1954, the Curve Lake First Nations community elected the first woman chief in Canada.

Elsie agreed to run for office because there were many things about reserve life that she wanted to change, and she did not agree with legislation that gave the government total control over Native people. Her goals as chief were to improve access to good education, promote the Ojibwe language, and create the same opportunities for Native people that were

Chief Elsie Marie Knott.

available to non-Natives. She lost no time in moving her agenda forward.

As a young woman, Elsie was shy and withdrawn, but as she grew older and faced the challenges of being the bread-winner for her family, she began to believe in herself. Her personality blossomed, and she became an approachable and outgoing person. She recognized the value in telling a good joke and not taking herself too seriously. Her success in developing Knott's Bus Service, her involvement in the com-munity, and the trust her community had in her all bolstered her confidence. Interaction with her band made her realize the importance of being inclusive—bringing everyone into the decision-making process and getting them involved so they feel they are a part of what is happening. One of the first things

Elsie did after being elected chief was to bring back the community powwow. The event brought the community together to celebrate their culture, and it opened the reserve's culture and traditions for non-Natives to experience. In addition, the money raised from the event helped fund Christmas for needy families in the community.

With her well-designed plans, fun-loving personality, and ability to motivate, Elsie never seemed to have problems with the many ventures she put forward. She was in continuous motion, presenting ideas for projects and following through until they were finished. Some of her accomplishments were negotiating with the government for funds to build forty-five new houses, digging new wells for better water access, and paving roads on the reserve to replace the gravel tracks she drove every day for so many years. She was also responsible for bringing a grocery store, post office, day-care center, and senior citizens' home to the community. All of these achievements were important to her, but she was especially proud of the day-care center. She saw that project as the ticket to a better life for many families. Mothers like her who had to work would now have affordable, reliable childcare while they sought employment or furthered their education. She also knew from experience what it was like to not feel empowered as a woman. To lift women up in her band, she organized the Curve Lake Indian Homemakers Association. This club became a center for political activism for Native women and gave reserve women the opportunity to discuss women's issues and community politics.

Elsie faced many challenges among her successes. One of her biggest disappointments came in 1976, when she lost her last campaign for reelection. After serving for sixteen years, in two different cycles, she was defeated in her eighth race for chief. She was devastated, and her trust in the community was rocked. She felt betrayed. But, as good leaders do, Elsie rebounded to live out her years as one of the most respected and admired people from the Curve Lake First Nations band.

Elsie believed education and cultural knowledge are the backbone of a strong Native community. Preserving and promoting the Ojibwe language was a priority for her, and she would visit jails and teach the language to prisoners. Elsie was instrumental in starting an Ojibwe language program at the Curve Lake First Nations School, with her daughter, Rita, serving as the language instructor.

Elsie did not shy away from controversy, either. Her disgust with the 1969 White Paper on Indian Policy resulted in her publicly burning the document, then dancing on the ashes. On another occasion, in 1975, Elsie led a protest against provincial legislation that encroached on Indian treaty rights to hunt and fish. Again, she was a staunch advocate for her Native people, standing up and fighting against the injustice.

Elsie Marie Knott made her mark not only as the first woman chief of a First Nations band but also as a powerful and compassionate leader. She left this world on December 3, 1995, recognized for so many accomplishments for the First Nations people. As Chief Dalton Jacobs stated, "She was someone with tenacity and a strong work ethic. She would have done well in any community, but I am just happy that she was part of my community."

AWARDS AND HONORS

- Life Achievement Award, Union of Ontario Indians, 1999
- Anishinabek Nation's Celebration of Women Conference honoree, 1998
- Outstanding Women Award, 1992
- Minister of Indian Affairs award for twenty-five years of accident-free school bus driving, 1980

- *Elsie, Indian Chief, Bus Driver, Shopkeeper, Grannie*, a play about Elsie written by Lois Franks, 1980
- Ontario's Twenty-Five Outstanding Women, International Women's Year, 1975

Mary Golda Ross

CHEROKEE

She was a strong-willed, independent woman who was ahead of her time. And a proud woman who never forgot where she was from.

NORBERT HILL

 s darkness falls and twilight turns into the night sky, have you ever lain on your back in the cool, damp grass and stared at the starry sky above? Many years ago, a young Cherokee girl from the state of Oklahoma had dreams of her own that had an incredible impact on how we view the stars, moon, and planets above.

Mary Golda Ross was born on August 9, 1908, a time when girls grew into women who were trained to manage a household. If they were lucky enough to attend school, they were guided toward more genteel, acceptable subjects, such as reading, spelling, history, geography, and handwriting. They also learned manners and how to walk "like a lady." In a typical American classroom at that time, girls were not encouraged to pursue subjects such as math, biology, and other sciences. Young women were expected to learn how to best keep house and raise their children. But this was not the case with Mary Golda Ross.

Mary was born into the Cherokee Indian tribe in Oklahoma. Her family embraced their tribal beliefs, which valued

79

Mary receiving the Eagle Feather award.

education equally among girls and boys. As Mary was growing up, her parents saw that their child was very talented and smart, and they wanted her to have the best schooling available. They made the difficult decision to bear the absence of their daughter in order to give her the opportunities of public schooling not available in their town. Mary's grandparents lived in Tahlequah, Oklahoma, about six miles from her hometown of Park Hill, so they sent Mary to her grandparents to live throughout the ten years of her primary and secondary education. Later, Mary attributed her successes to the rich heritage of her Cherokee people and the importance of tribal emphasis on education. "I was brought up in the Cherokee tradition of equal education for boys and girls," she said. "It did not bother me to be the only girl in the math class . . . math was more fun than anything else. It was always a game to me." Why shouldn't people pursue the thing in life that makes them happy? Mary flourished in her early years of schooling and relished the opportunities that lay ahead as she moved forward in learning and excelling in her studies.

What was Mary's life like as she was growing up? The state of Oklahoma was as newborn as Mary Ross, since it only became a state in 1907. The Ross family had long and deep roots in the making of what was first referred to as "Indian Territory," which later became Oklahoma. An important player in this transition was Chief John Ross, Mary's great-great-grandfather. Many years before, he led the Cherokee Nation on the tragic Trail of Tears march in 1838, a forced migration from the southeastern United States to the Cherokees' final home in Oklahoma. More than four thousand Cherokee people died during this march, which took more than three months and covered one thousand miles through the dead of winter. Chief John Ross was so revered as a leader that he later became the longest-serving chief of the Cherokee people.

After settling his family in Park Hill, Oklahoma, Chief John Ross focused on establishing his family's new home on the values of the Cherokee way, particularly the importance of education. As chief, he helped establish the first institution of higher learning west of the Mississippi in 1850, the Cherokee National Female Seminary. The coursework emphasized the sciences, with classes in botany, chemistry, and physics. He even built his own library to ensure access to literature. Benefiting from access to the school built by her great-great-grandfather, Mary completed her high school education in Tahlequah at the age of sixteen. She then returned home to her family in Park Hill to attend Northeastern State Teachers College (now Northeastern State University).

This emphasis on education continued throughout several generations of Rosses. Mary's father was trained as a lawyer, and her aunts were all schoolteachers. Her mother also donated land for the school grounds. "My parents believed an education was necessary to make something of yourself," Mary said. "So from childhood, I had been encouraged to get the best education possible and make the most of my opportunities. I did not dare miss a day of school." That drive to succeed resulted in Mary's receiving her bachelor's degree in mathematics in 1928. She was ready to join the work world.

When Mary Ross entered the job market, there were few opportunities for women to use their college education for anything other than teaching, but she lost no time in putting her degree to work. Mary began teaching math and science in nearby high schools. She spent the next nine years dedicated to giving her students the same learning opportunities she had been given.

Although Mary took pride in her teaching, she had started asking herself whether she was going to venture out and see anything of the world or stay in northern Oklahoma. The towns where she had been teaching were small and the social life was limited for a young, single woman. Later, she reflected on her life without regret: "I never married. . . . I was teaching in little schools, where you didn't have many dates. And by the time I came out where I could meet more people, they were all at war or getting married on furlough." Her work and social life were full and busy, and she had no time for marriage.

Mary was twenty-nine years old and had never been farther from Park Hill than her grandparents' home six miles away. But travel she did. This motivated and curious woman applied for work as a statistical clerk for the Bureau of Indian Affairs in Washington, DC. She held this position for a short period of time before she was encouraged to pursue a very different route. "There was a Cherokee woman in the Department of Education who asked me to come over," Mary said. "She told me, 'We can't waste you here. You're an Indian girl with a degree and experience in teaching. We need you out in the field.' So I was sent to Santa Fe, New Mexico." The interest this woman showed in Mary impressed upon her the value of someone recognizing your potential and providing advocacy and mentoring.

In November 1937, Mary settled into her new life in New Mexico, an area rich in Native American culture. The pueblos; the arts representing some of the best in pottery, jewelry making, and weaving; and the beautiful landscape surrounding her were impressive. Mary worked as a girls' adviser at the Santa Fe Indian School, a boarding school that later became the Institute of American Indian Arts. Teaching at a boarding school meant that most students went home over the summer. This allowed Mary to work hard during that time to complete a master's degree in math at the University of

Mary awarding a scholarship in her name.

Northern Colorado. Again, Mary was often the only woman in her math classes, but that didn't seem to bother her. She stated, "I was the only female in my class. I sat on one side of the room and the guys on the other side. . . . I guess they didn't want to associate with me. But I could hold my own with them, and sometimes I did better." She completed her master's degree in mathematics a year later. However, during this time another area of science caught her attention. She developed a keen interest in astronomy (the study of the sun, moon, stars, planets, comets, and other celestial bodies). She read every book on the subject she could get her hands on.

Mary had been in Santa Fe five years when a Christmas vacation trip to California triggered an incident that had a profound effect on her life. The activities set into motion a chain of events that would transform this small-town teacher into a big-time participant in the exploration of space. "There wasn't much use at the school [in Santa Fe] for my technical training," she said. World War II was going at this time, and her friends told her of a large company in California that was in need of people with a technical education. Mary decided to apply and was on the job at Lockheed Aircraft Corporation by July 1, 1942. This is where the real story of Mary Golda Ross begins.

Lockheed Aircraft Corporation in Burbank, California, got its start building seaplanes. It would later build aircraft that would break speed and distance records and carry men and women to outer space. Mary began her career at Lockheed as a mathematician's assistant. She was one of many, but it didn't take long for her to stand out among her peers.

During World War II, many women joined the workforce outside the home and provided important support in factories and companies that contributed to the United States winning the war. Most able-bodied young men were drafted to serve in the military, and there was a shortage of men to fill positions. But as these soldiers came back home, women were fired from their jobs to allow the men to return to work. Remember, at this time men were considered the "breadwinners" for the family and women were expected to stay home and tend the household. Although Mary was in a male-dominated field, in a position that typically would have gone back to a man, Lockheed saw in her the intelligence and skills that would benefit the company far into the future. Not only was she kept in her position but she also was offered an opportunity to become an engineer. Intensive training followed in math and aeronautical engineering on the job and through the emergency war training courses. Mary also took evening classes at the University of California, Los Angeles (UCLA). Of this time in her life, Mary said, "I took the opportunity, studied on the job, and went to school, and within about a year and a half I had qualified. It was hard, a lot of plodding, but I've always been curious to learn." In 1949, Ross received her first professional engineering credential as a mechanical engineer, since there was no aeronautical college degree in the state of California at that time.

Mary's talents were quickly recognized, and she rapidly progressed beyond being a mathematician's assistant. In 1952, she became the only woman, and the only Native American, asked to join an elite group of forty engineers called the Skunk Works, a top secret team whose work helped launch Lockheed Missiles and Space Company. Much of the work done by this group still remains classified (top secret), but there is much to be noted in the contributions Mary Ross made to the field of aeronautics and space travel. At this time, there were a handful of women like Mary who worked in various scientific fields, but little was known about them. The work of amazing women who were early trailblazers in scientific discoveries is finally being recognized in movies like *Hidden Figures*.

Ross worked on the forefront of space technology as part of planning teams for missions to Mars, Venus, and the outer

planets of the solar system. The Agena rocket project record-
ed many spaceflight firsts and was an essential step in the
Apollo program to land a man on the moon. This was a major
endeavor and a critical leap for America's space program.
Mary's accomplishments in rocket science and aeronautics
were significant and numerous, from providing early design
concepts for space travel between planets to determining the
effects of air pressure on the Lockheed P-38 Lightning, one of
the fastest airplanes designed at the time.

After spending thirty-one remarkable years at Lockheed,
Mary retired and stepped into a new chapter in her life. Perhaps she remembered back thirty-seven years to that woman
at the Bureau of Indian Affairs, the person who recognized her
talent and encouraged her to challenge herself to seek new
horizons. Certainly, her Cherokee upbringing and her belief
in the power of education influenced her too. She became a
strong advocate for encouraging Native American youth to get
an education, and, in particular, was a staunch supporter
of young women in engineering and science. The majority of
Mary's life was spent working
and interacting with people far
away from her Oklahoma roots,
and she once shared that one of
the few regrets she had was that
she spent so much of her life
apart from Indian people. This
could have been why, in her
retirement years, she dedicated herself to three causes: the
American Indian Science and
Engineering Society, the Council of Energy Resource Tribes,
and the Smithsonian Institution's National Museum of the
American Indian (to which she
donated more than $400,000

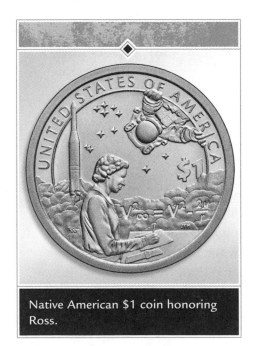

Native American $1 coin honoring
Ross.

of her life savings). Her influence is evident in the feelings expressed by the recipients of scholarships granted in her name. One recipient wrote: "The Mary G. Ross Scholarship has helped me tremendously, not only financially contributing to my education but also by affirming that someone believes I have the skills to be successful in the engineering field."

Mary Ross led a full life that touched and influenced many. Her keen intellect sparked curiosity and demanded respect. Her self-motivation and pride in her Cherokee heritage was evident even into her last years. For the special occasion of the grand opening of the National Museum of the American Indian, she asked her niece to make her a traditional Cherokee dress, the first she had ever owned. On a sunny September 21, 2004, ninety-six-year-old Mary Ross joined twenty-five thousand other Indigenous people to celebrate this momentous event. In the opening procession, she stepped out of her wheelchair on the National Mall in Washington, DC, and walked for half a block. "She felt she was a part of history being made again," said friend Norbert Hill. Mary Golda Ross died four years later on April 29, 2008, just three months short of her one-hundredth birthday, but her legacy lives on in the inspiration, advocacy, and contributions she made that positively influence countless lives today.

AWARDS AND HONORS

- Featured on the Native American US dollar coin, US Mint, 2019
- Featured on Google Doodle, honoring her achievements, August 9, 2018
- Women of Achievement Award in Science and Technology, The Women's Fund, 1994
- Trailblazer Award, University of Northern Colorado Alumni Association, 1993
- Inducted into the Silicon Valley Engineering Council's Hall of Fame, 1992

- Ely S. Parker Award, AISES, 1985
- Eagle Feather Award from the Council of Energy Resource Tribes, 1985
- Honorary Life Membership Award, American Indian Science and Engineering Society, 1984
- The Santa Clara Valley Section, Society of Women Engineers, established a scholarship in her name, 1973
- Woman of Distinction Award, *San Francisco Examiner*, 1961
- Women of Achievement Award, California State Federation of Business and Professional Women's Clubs, 1961
- Matrix Table Award for Space Age Communication of Ideas, Theta Sigma Phi, 1961
- Fellow and life member, Society of Women Engineers

Heather Dawn Thompson

LAKOTA, CHEYENNE RIVER SIOUX

In our every deliberation, we must consider the impact of our decisions on the next seven generations.

IROQUOIS MAXIM

 Heather Dawn Thompson is an attorney who has lived in countries around the world, led national organizations, and always maintained the stalwart nature that exemplifies the roots of generations before her. She was born on September 22, 1971, in Langdon, North Dakota, to Keith and Cleo (Dolphus) Thompson. Heather is the fourth-removed great-granddaughter of the Lakota Sioux couple Red Dressing and One Iron Horn. Their daughter, Good Elk Woman, married a French Canadian, Frederick Dupree, and they had nine children. (At various times, Fred-

Heather Dawn Thompson.

89

erick's surname was spelled Dupuis, Dupree, DuPriest, and Dupri, but Dupree is the spelling on his tombstone.) Their youngest child, Marcella, married Douglas F. Carlin in 1879 and, due to the prominence of the Dupree family, the wedding was a social event so notable that it was reported in two statewide newspapers in South Dakota. An abundance of wedding gifts were received, the most impressive being five hundred head of cattle and fifty horses from the bride's father, Fred. Fred Dupree is also remembered for saving the buffalo from certain extinction in the early 1880s due to the wanton slaughter of the vast herds that roamed the prairies at that time. Heather's great-great-grandfather Carlin later became a state senator in South Dakota. With this family background, it is no surprise that Heather Dawn Thompson has respect for those around her and a desire to serve the Native people.

Heather's childhood was filled with travel and multicultural experiences, which she credits for her ability to adapt quickly and work effectively with diverse communities. Her father worked for an international construction company that kept their family on the move, traveling to where the next job was located. Heather attended schools and traveled or lived in more than forty countries, which gave her a unique perspective on working in different cultures. These experiences helped mold her into the confident, effective leader that she is today.

Heather's early education was spent in countries as diverse as Holland, Saudi Arabia, the Philippines, and many others. She enjoyed school and was a good student, but living abroad was not always easy for her and her brother. Moving so often meant that she only had one year, maybe two, to settle into the educational process and make friends. A particularly challenging time was when her family relocated from San Diego, California, to the Philippines. She remembers how they went from a very affluent lifestyle to witnessing abject poverty in the country to which they had just moved.

Heather with relatives at the grand opening of the National Museum of the American Indian, 2004.

The adjustment was difficult but proved to be her first life lesson in cultural awareness. Heather says, "People are the same everywhere. You'll find good people and bad people wherever you are. It's up to you to learn to work with the differences." She developed her people skills in order to make friends and meet the challenges.

Heather was born with a sense of individualism. She was fearless when she latched on to an idea and was relentless in seeing it through. While living in South Korea during her middle-school years, Heather was determined to attend a sporting event her friends were participating in hundreds of miles away from her home in Seoul. Unable to accompany her, Heather's parents said no to her request to go. But the determined girl planned the trip and then convinced Keith and Cleo that she would be fine. With a note in hand, which she was to give to the taxi driver who would take her to the stadium, Heather waved goodbye to her parents, boarded the south-bound train, and made it there and back home successfully. Her mother says, "As the train pulled away, Keith and I looked at each other and said, 'What kind of parents would allow their thirteen-year-old girl to do this?'"

Heather at graduation, Harvard University, Harvard Law School.

But they knew their daughter. They recognized the need to allow her to be independent and not be afraid to be who she is.

After finishing high school, Heather attended the University of Florida and Carnegie Mellon University before completing her law degree at Harvard University. Her prior work experience helped shape her commitment to the Native people. While studying at Harvard, she became very aware of how the differences in culture and economic privilege affect educational opportunities. When Heather was working on her law degree (juris doctor), there were few universities in the country that included American Indian law in their coursework. Native students had difficulty relating their life experience growing up in a tribal environment to the discussions occurring in their classes. The tribal beliefs they shared were often not appreciated by their professors. Thus began Heather's passion to work with and for justice in Indian Country.

Heather's legal experience began with internships that included working with the Cheyenne River Sioux tribe, the Offices of the United States Attorneys, the District of Columbia, and Myron Orfield in the Minnesota House of Representatives. A number of factors figured into Heather's advocacy for Native people: her heritage, her upbringing in many different cultures, and, most significantly, her work in Washington, DC. Heather's many appointments included counsel and policy adviser for the US Senate and policy analyst for the US Immigration and Naturalization Services. About this time, she says,

"While working in DC, I saw the disproportionate impacts federal policy had on Indian people. Intellectually, you know the treaties specify that relationships are between the federal government and tribal nations. It is a different experience, though, when you see personally, on a day-to-day basis, the hugely impactful decisions that are made very casually at the federal level. These decisions that have giant, long-term consequences for Native people." Her time in Washington dramatically affected Heather's career path; she wanted to serve as an advocate on those issues with the federal government. So began the trajectory of one of the country's leading Native lawyers working in Indian Country.

Heather's work is broad based, which is important when fighting on behalf of Native Americans. In 2014, Heather, then the assistant attorney general for the state of South Dakota, led the investigation on a case that rocked the Pine Ridge Indian Reservation. Charles Chipps Sr. was a world-famous medicine man, traditional healer, and spiritual leader. Followers would travel long distances to his tiny village to be with him and pray in the darkness in sweat-lodge ceremonies. For years, this elderly tribal member gave counsel to those around him and was highly respected. But this holy man had a dark side that affected many lives.

Despite rumors throughout the years that Chipps was sexually abusing young women, there was very little action taken to look into the allegations. Then one day a very brave thirteen-year-old girl shared her story with her school counselor, who then was legally obligated to report what she had been told, and she did.

Heather Dawn Thompson had recently joined the US attorney's office in Rapid City. After her arrival, she soon became regarded as an expert in sexual-abuse cases because there were just so many to handle. "There are a variety of historical reasons that people point to for this cycle in Indian Country. One of which has to do with the federal policy of removing children from their homes and sending them to boarding schools during the late 1800s and much of the 1900s," Heather says. Many studies tie sexual abuse to the intergenerational trauma that began in these government- and church-run boarding schools. Court documents and lawsuit settlements reveal how the boarding schools, especially in places such as South Dakota, were centers of widespread sexual, emotional, and physical abuse. Many of the children who attended these schools are the parents and grandparents of today's Native American children.

Heather was personally familiar with the effects these schools had on Native people. Her maternal grandparents were products of the Indian boarding school system and her paternal grandparents ran their household by the adage "Spare the rod and spoil the child." Only as an adult did Heather become aware of the dysfunction and abuse that occurred in both her mother's and father's families as they grew up. Heather notes that she is most proud of her parents and their parenting because, she says, "They broke those cycles of abuse before that was even an articulated goal."

With the information provided by that brave young woman, the school counselor, and many more victims who came forward, Heather and a South Dakota FBI agent moved forward on the case. On July 16, 2013, a federal grand jury indicted (an indictment is a formal accusation that initiates a criminal case) Chipps on fifteen counts of rape, sexual abuse, and intimidation of six minors. In addition to the children in the indictment, older victims from South Dakota and other states came forward and alleged that they were also sexually abused by Chipps when they were younger. Unfortunately, Charles Chipps Sr. died awaiting trial. His victims did not get their day in court against their abuser, but Heather Dawn Thompson fought hard for justice on behalf of these women and girls.

In more recent years, Heather has focused on industry and economic development for business ventures in Indian Country. She speaks internationally on how to approach the cross-cultural issues related to tribal affairs and business start-ups.

Heather credits her early life of continued relocations for developing her ability to get along with people, as her job is now one of negotiating with tribes and white businesses and bridging their cultural differences.

One of the most pressing concerns on reservations is poor nutrition, mainly due to the lack of affordable fresh fruits and vegetables. Heather is leading an operation of indoor Native farms on the Pine Ridge Indian Reservation to provide a supply of fresh food for the tribe and to sell to off-reservation businesses, creating income for the tribe. This

The grand opening of the National Museum of the American Indian, 2004.

endeavor establishes access to hard-to-obtain fresh produce, providing healthier diets for a population that suffers from many diet-related illnesses, such as diabetes and heart disease.

Through all that she does, Heather demonstrates a strong belief in "her tribe," referring to all Native people, and emphasizes the importance of maintaining pride in Native language and culture. Her family life growing up made it difficult for her to connect with her Cheyenne River Indian tribe, but she recognized a deep desire for belonging. Heather is married to a Native man, and they have one son who was Lakota-adopted through the Hunka (child-beloved) rite, a kinship ceremony that is respected by all the family members involved. She finds comfort and familiarity in traditional Lakota teachings and ceremonies, and her spiritual beliefs are centered on the Lakota core principles. She and her husband attend *yuwipi* and *inipi*, the healing and purification rites of the Lakota people.

Heather Dawn Thompson is a tireless crusader for doing what is right for Native people. She believes that the key to their future success is in the hands of today's Native youth, as they must learn their tribal language and preserve their culture. Her advice to them is spoken with the unvarnished truth of someone who has directly witnessed the injustices faced by Native people: "The path ahead is fixed against you. If it feels like it's hard, it's because it is! It's harder to find opportunities, but acknowledge these impediments and move forward. Don't let them win!"

AWARDS AND HONORS

- Listed, "The Best Lawyers in America, Native American Law," bestlawyers.com, 2020
- Founder, Lakota Language Classroom Preschool Program, 2013
- Board member, Cheyenne River Youth Project Advisory Board, 2001–present
- Team member, "2016 Hot List: Indian Law Practitioners," *Indian Country Today*, 2016
- Selected, "Top Lawyers in Native American Law," 5280.com, 2015 and 2016
- Cofounder and past president, South Dakota Indian Country Bar Association, 2011
- Member, Native American Federal Judicial Nomination Committee, 2009–2011
- Creator and national coordinator, Native Vote Election Protection, 2004–2010
- President, National Native American Bar Association, 2007–2009
- Deputy chair, Federal Bar Association, Indian Law Section, 2006–2008

Emily Washines

YAKAMA NATION WITH CREE
AND SKOKOMISH LINEAGE

This is a story of hope as much as it is of history.

EMILY WASHINES

The house lights dimmed and the drumming started. Members from hundreds of tribes across the
United States and Canada listened to a *waushat*
song being sung by two elders of the Yakama Nation. It was
a warrior song that young Emily Washines recognized, but
why was it being sung for her? Their song and drumming
ended, and Emily was honored as she listened to one of the
elders, who leaned forward to quietly say, "Pageants were
just as tough as going into battle." Those words provided a
welcome boost of confidence, especially for someone who was
about to be crowned Miss National Congress of American
Indians (NCAI) in 1999.

Emily Washines was born in 1981 in a small town in central Washington State. The city of Toppenish sits on the
Yakama Indian reservation and is the headquarters for the
Yakama Nation. Emily and her four siblings were brought
up in a home that valued the traditions, culture, and language
of the Yakama people. Her parents, Archie and Stella, made
sure their children recognized the value of their culture and

language and were exposed to them. Powwows and traditional crafts, such as beading and basketmaking, were woven into the Washines children's upbringing.

Emily's large extended family was well known for its involvement in the community. Learning Ichiskiin Sinwit (Yakama language), being competitive in softball, and following the traditions of her tribe were all part of her makeup. So when a few of the tribal elders encouraged her to compete in the Indian pageants, Emily seized an opportunity to show respect for her elders and represent the Yakama Nation. This pride in her people led her to first run for Miss Yakama Nation and then Miss NCAI, winning both pageants. The respect she had for the tribal elders motivated her, and she heeded their advice: "Never forget the role of women in this tribe. Women were in our wars." From that moment on, Emily has taken this message forward and allowed it to direct the course of her life.

Emily recognizes the value of education and has made it a priority in her life, as a student and as a teacher. With two bachelor's degrees and a master's degree, Emily has used her education in a variety of ways. She is a firm believer that learning outside of the classroom is as important as learning inside of it. Her extracurricular activities in college included traveling to Alaska to study the language preservation of the Native tribes there. She also worked for the governor of Washington State for three months as an education intern, promoting literacy programs. This experience contributed to her ability to effectively work and communicate with diverse communities.

With a deep respect for knowledge and learning, Emily focused her early career on encouraging students to pursue a college degree. As an admissions counselor at her alma mater, Central Washington University, she had the opportunity to show Native students that higher education was possible for them. She was proof that, through persistence and hard work, they could make a better life for themselves and take that knowledge back to their tribes.

Emily Washines.

After seven years of working with students, Emily found her way back to the classroom as a student, this time to complete a master's degree in public administration. In the commencement speech she gave at The Evergreen State College upon receiving her master's, she noted that she had accomplished the completion of three degrees and the birth of two children in eight years. Her introduction to the stage that day included that "her eight-month-old daughter has spent her whole life in graduate school!"

Emily's education and experience contributed to the skill set that has benefited her work preserving tribal culture and advocating for the murdered and missing women and girls of the Yakama Nation. With the words of her elders still ringing in her ears, Emily is fulfilling her promise to tell that story of the strong women of the Yakama, the story of the women warriors, who, in the past and into the future, are the strength of the tribe.

Emily's story is as much rooted in bygone centuries as it is in the present. She lives on land that was known as the Washington Territory in 1855. The Native Americans who resided there had been in talks with the United States government, negotiating a treaty that would lead to peaceful relations with the white people who were moving onto their ancestral lands. And then things went terribly wrong. A rewrite of history, the correcting of events, is where Emily's energy is focused.

The situations that occurred on this land many years ago reflect the treatment of Native women today. On a sunny autumn afternoon in 1855, a mother and her daughter, with her tiny baby on a cradleboard, were walking the hills around their home, digging roots and gathering herbs that would sustain them through the long winter ahead. All at once they were attacked by a group of white men, miners who were traveling through to work the gold fields north of the territory. Upon finding his murdered family, the Native husband tracked the men and killed them. What followed next is what history books cite as the cause of the Yakama War—the killing of the miners and a government Indian agent. But the Yakama people know better. The war began with the violation and death of Native women. This tragedy is not lost on Emily Washines, and she carries that connection through to the tragedy that Native women and girls now face every day.

The silent cries of murdered and missing Indigenous women are finally getting a voice.

Growing up on an Indian reservation can be dangerous. Mothers remind their daughters each time they leave the house to be careful because bad things have happened "out there" to their sisters, or mothers, or aunties. The saddest part is that for years no one in authority seemed to care. Across the United States and Canada, thousands of women and girls have been murdered or are missing. And this is where Emily's work circles back to the event that started the 1855 Yakama War and her promise to her elders. Strong warrior women of the Yakama Nation are taking up the fight to be heard, to pass legislation to protect Native people, and to hold accountable those who disrespect them.

The trauma associated with any violation of the mind or body is destructive. To provide sanctuary and guidance toward healing and learning, Emily created the website and blog Native Friends. This Native-focused site shares thoughts and information about Native history and culture, with the aim of building understanding and support for Native Americans.

Among the many resources found on the Native Friends website is a reference to Emily's work with the Enduring Legacies Native Cases Initiative, whose mission is to provide culturally relevant lesson plans and teaching material for students. The initiative is sponsored by The Evergreen State College, in partnership with other institutions. The restoration of culture and language are paramount to Emily's work, and she also emphasizes the importance of food and its connection to the land and to nature.

In the Native American culture, food has always been of central importance, not only for the livelihood of the people but also as a tool for teaching language and tradition. As a young girl, Emily remembers joining her family at the Satus Shaker Church on the Yakama Reservation. She recalls how her *ala* ("grandmother" in the Ichiskiin Sinwit language) would begin the meal with a prayer and a song. As the meal started, the food would be brought out in a specific order and placed on the table. Once all the dishes were presented, everyone would *choosh* (take a drink of water), then the eating would begin. The menu of dishes might include salmon, deer, elk, and fresh berries, which are all traditional foods. But one of the food items missing from the Yakama table until recently was the *wapato* (potato). This vegetable was in abundance on the tribal lands until stream and river diversions caused the area to dry up. In the 1970s, the Yakama Nation made the decision to restore a portion of the reservation to its original wetlands status, and with that decision, much of the natural vegetation returned. The wapato returned to the Yakama table as a traditional dish. Emily regularly harvests and promotes the wapato as part of the culture of the tribe, as seen in her film *Return of the Wapato: Natural Restoration and Cultural Knowledge.*

Emily and her husband, Jon Shellenberger, have worked hard to instill that cultural connection to the land in their children. They have learned that food offers sustenance and traditional medicine, which keep the people healthy and wholesome. Emily carries this message through her films, writing, speaking engagements, and exhibits, all of which highlight Native culture, tradition, and language.

In every aspect of her life, Emily has demonstrated what strong Native women can be. To her students, she is inspiration. To her daughters and young Native girls, she is a role model. And to her tribe, she is the voice that can help right the many wrongs that have happened to Native people for centuries.

On that stage at the Miss NCAI pageant in 1999, Emily Washines was expected to provide a talent presentation. She did not sing a song or dance to music. Instead, she read a poem, one that she had written to show her pride in her Native people and her hope for the Yakama Nation. In part, she recited in Ichiskiin Sinwit and English: "I know that my people's future isn't doomed, knowing I wanted to change, feeling endowed to my ancestors." She is keeping her promise to her elders and is diligent in protecting the legacy of the strong women warriors of the Yakama.

AWARDS AND HONORS

- Board member, Artist Trust, Washington State
- Board member, Columbia Riverkeepers
- Single Impact Event Award, Association of King County Historical Organizations, 2018
- Cover article, "Return of the Wapato," *The Evergreen Magazine*, 2018
- Advisory board member, Museum of Culture and Environment, 2017–present
- *Yakima Herald-Republic* Top 39 under 39, 2020
- Miss Indian World, first runner-up, 2000
- *The Silence Within: Crevices at Tribes*, short film screened at One Heart Native Arts and Film Festival, 2017
- CWU board of trustees, Central Washington University, 2017
- Crowned Miss Yakama Nation, 1999
- Crowned Miss National Congress of American Indians, 1999

Chapter 1

"Ashley Callingbull, Full Biography." Ashley Callingbull website. Retrieved May 25, 2020. https://ashleycallingbullofficial.com/biography.

"Ashley Callingbull—A Survivor Story." NewJourneys.ca., September 26, 2018. https://www.newjourneys.ca/en/articles/ashley-callingbull-a-survivor-story.

"Ashley Callingbull." Miss Universe Canada. Retrieved May 26, 2020. https://missuniversecanada.ca/2013-national-finalists/ashley-callingbull.

"Ashley Callingbull." REDx Talks Preview, November 24, 2015. https://www.youtube.com/watch?v=c8hDvnOjNiw.

Boesveld, Sarah. "'I'm Not Going to Shut Up': First Nations Woman Crowned Mrs. Universe Urges Canadians to Vote for New PM." *National Post*, September 1, 2015. https://nationalpost.com/news/canada/first-nations-woman-crowned-mrs-universe-urges-canadians-to-vote-for-new-pm.

Dean, Flannery. "Meet Ashley Callingbull-Burnham, Badass Beauty Queen." *Flare Magazine*. September 16, 2015. https://www.flare.com/tv-movies/meet-ashley-callingbull-burnham-canadas-badass-beauty-queen.

Holt, David. "Ashley Callingbull; Fearless Fighter." *Life*, November 15, 2019. https://www.optimyz.com/mrs-universe-ashley-callingbull-interview.

Hune-Brown, Nicholas. "All Hail Ashley Callingbull: From 'Pageant Girl' to Powerhouse." *Chatelaine*, December 7, 2015. https://www.chatelaine.com/living/features-living/all-hail-mrs-universe-ashley-callingbull.

Montiel, Anya. "Thoshography: The Fashion Photography of Thosh Collins." National Museum of the American Indian. Fall 2013.

Morin, Brandi. "Rising Enoch Actress/Model Overcomes Stereotypes and Adversity." *Spruce Grove Examiner*. Thursday, January 12, 2012.

"The Canadian Mrs. Universe Winner Is All Kinds of Amazing." *Flare Magazine*, September 1, 2015. https://www.flare.com/beauty/canadian-mrs-universe-winner-ashley-callingbull-is-all-kinds-of-amazing.

White, Samantha. "Former Mrs. Universe Ashley Callingbull on Speaking Out through Style Social Sharing." *CBC Life*, June 21, 2018. https://www.cbc.ca/life/style/former-mrs-universe-ashley-callingbull-on-speaking-out-through-style-1.4715928.

Chapter 2

"Biography of Dr. Henrietta Mann." Native American Student Advocacy Institute, College Board. Retrieved June 3, 2020. https://nasai.collegeboard.org/about.

Durmen, Kimberley. "Dr. Henrietta Mann / Cheyenne / Distinguished Educator / Founding Member of the AISES Council of Elders." *Winds of Change*, American Indian Science and Engineering Society, October 21, 2019. https://Woc.Aises.Org/2019-Fall-Issue.

"Henrietta Mann, Biographical Interview." Cheyenne Arapaho College. January 8, 2014. Audio 7:22. https://www.youtube.com/watch?v=PuczDp6hgqU.

Hertzel, David. 2017. *Ancestors: Who We Are and Where We Come From*. Rowman & Littlefield, London, pp. 4–13.

Mann, Dr. Henrietta. "Hoosta-oo-nah'e, 'The Woman Who Comes to Offer Prayer' or 'Prayer Woman.'" *Distinctly Montana*, March 12, 2019. https://www.distinctlymontana.com/mann192.

Schmidt, Carol. "Henrietta Mann." Montana State University, April 2, 2007. Retrieved http://www.montana.edu/news/mountainsandminds/article.html?id=9303.

Schmidt, Carol. "The Passion of Henrietta Mann." *Indian Country Today*, vol. 3, issue 24 (2016). https://ictmn.lughstudio.com/wp-content/uploads/2016/06/E-weekly-24-Archives-ICTMN-1.pdf.

Schmidt, Carol. "At 82, Henrietta Mann Remains Busy Promoting American Indian Education." *Indian Country Today*, June 4, 2016. https://indiancountrytoday.com/archive/at-82-henrietta-mann-remains-busy-promoting-american-indian-education-MXHAdffJzUuhJ-VBRhdMhQ.

Schontzler, Gail. "Henrietta Mann Blazes a Trail for N.A.'s." *Bozeman Chronicle*, January 27, 2001. https://www.bozemandailychronicle.com/henrietta-mann-blazes-a-trail-for-n-a-s/article_7864b538-3bfc-5d1f-ac60-0ee37d94d2d1.html.

"SWOSU Dedicates Mann Hall in Honor of Dr. Henrietta Mann." *Cheyenne and Arapaho Tribal Tribune*, December 1, 2018, vol. 14, issue 23. https://cheyenneandarapaho-nsn.gov/wp-content/uploads/2018/12/Dec.-1-2018.pdf.

Wright, Russ. "Commend Dr. Henrietta Mann for Work to Preserve Native American Culture." *Cheyenne and Arapaho Tribal Tribune*, February 12, 2020. https://cheyennearapahotribaltribune.word press.com/2020/02/12/wright-russ-commend-dr-henrietta-mann-for-work-to-preserve-native-american-culture.

Chapter 3

Astor, Maggie. "Meet the Native American Woman Who Beat the Sponsor of North Dakota's ID Law." *New York Times*, November 13, 2018. https://www.nytimes.com/2018/11/13/us/politics/north-dakota-ruth-buffalo.html.

Beck, Abaki. "Why Aren't Fossil Fuel Companies Held Accountable for Missing and Murdered Indigenous Women?" *Yes!* Solutions Journalism. October 5, 2019. https://www.yesmagazine.org/environment/2019/10/05/native-fossil-fuel-missing-murdered-indigenous-women-mmiwg.

"Near Spill, Reservation Wrestles with Oil's Impact." *Korea Herald*, July 15, 2014. http://nwww.koreaherald.com.

Nichols, John. "How a Native American Woman Defeated a 4-Term Republican Incumbent." *The Nation*, September 17, 2019. https://www.thenation.com/podcast/politics/north-dakota-ruth-anna-buffalo.

"Ruth Buffalo." *Indigenous Goddess Gang*, December 10, 2018. https://www.indigenousgoddessgang.com/matriarch-monday/2018/12/9/ruth-buffalo.

"Ruth Anna Buffalo." Freedom Road LLC. Retrieved May 7, 2020. Https://Freedomroad.Us/Who-We-Are/Ruth-Anna-Buffalo/Ruth Anna Buffalo.

"Ruth Buffalo, Biography." Vote Smart, Facts Matter. Retrieved May 6, 2020. https://justfacts.votesmart.org/candidate/biography/181405/ruth-buffalo

Buffalo, Ruth, Speaker Profile. Netroots Nation. Retrieved May 6, 2020. https://www.netrootsnation.org/profile/ruth-buffalo.

Rivas, Mekita. "The First Native Woman Democrat in North Dakota Wore Traditional Regalia to Be Sworn-In." *Teen Vogue*, December

5, 2018. https://www.teenvogue.com/story/ruth-buffalo-first-native-woman-democrat-north-dakota-traditional-regalia-sworn-in.

Sorensen, Sally Jo. "North Dakota State Rep Ruth Buffalo Introduces Bills to Improve State's Response to MMIW." Weblog post. *Bluestem Prairie* blog, Maynard: Newstex. January 9, 2019.

Sunuwar, Dev Kumar. Buffalo, Ruth Anna, "Indigenous Women Face Multiple Challenges Says Ruth Anna Buffalo." *Dev Hammer Show*, Episode 13, Indigenous Television. May 17, 2018. https://www.youtube.com/watch?v=pP4t7uuSD_Q&feature=share.

Whiting, Lonna. "Ruth Anna Buffalo: Woman of the Year." HPR, October 2, 2019. https://hpr1.com/index.php/feature/news/ruth-anna-buffalo-woman-of-the-year.

Chapter 4

Berger, Bethany. Elouise Cobell: Bringing the United States to Account. *"Our Cause Will Ultimately Triumph": Profiles from the American Indian Sovereignty Movement* (Tim Alan Garrison, ed., Carolina Academic Press, 2014, pp. 192–195).

Cobell, Eloise. "Accounting Fiasco Result of Government Myth-Weaving." *Indian Country Today.* December 19, 2007.

Flynn, Johnnie P. "If You Can't Beat 'Em, Cheat 'Em." *Indian Country Today*, December 11, 2002. http://ezp.lib.cwu.edu/login?url=https://searchproquestcom.ezp.lib.cwu.edu/docview/362607038?accountid=10389.

Goodman, Lawrence. "A Daughter's Birthright." *Ladies' Home Journal*, vol. 122, issue 2 (2005): 148.

Grant, Anne des Rosier. "100 Years: One Woman's Fight for Justice." Model Teaching Unit, Montana Office of Public Instruction, 2017.

Hevesi, Dennis, "Elouise Cobell, 65, Dies; Sued U.S. Over Indian Trust Funds." *New York Times*, October 17, 2011. https://www.nytimes.com/2011/10/18/us/elouise-cobell-65-dies-sued-us-over-indian-trust-funds.html.

Johansen, Bruce E. "Cobell, Elouise." In *American Indian Biographies*, rev. ed., edited by Carole A. Barrett, Harvey J. Markowitz, and R. Kent Rasmussen, 99–102. Pasadena, CA: Salem Press, 2005.

Leonnig, Carol D. "Straight Shooter to Some, Loose Cannon to Others: [FINAL Edition]." *Washington Post*, September 15, 2005. http://ezp.lib.cwu.edu/login?url=https://search-proquest-com.ezp.lib.cwu.edu/docview/410006414?accountid=10389.

O'Brien, Edward. 2019. "Montana Honors Memory of Blackfeet Activist Elouise Cobell," Montana Public Radio, November 4, 2019. https://www.mtpr.org/post/montana-honors-memory-blackfeet-activist-elouise-cobell.

Volz, Matt. "Elouise Cobell Dies in Montana." *Native Times*, October 17, 2011. https://nativetimes.com/current-news/49-life/people/6193-elouise-cobell-dies-in-montana271.

Whitty, Julia. "Elouise Cobell's Accounting Coup." *Mother Jones*, September/October 2005. https://www.motherjones.com/politics/2005/09/accounting-coup-0.

Chapter 5

"ALA Prez Accused of Abetting Censorship." *School Library Journal* vol. 53, issue 12 (2007): 15. https://search-ebscohostcom. Ezp.lib.cw.edu/login.aspx?direct=true&db=a9h&AN=29360782 &site=ehost-live.

Goodes, Pamela A. "New ALA President Loriene Roy to Focus on Literacy, Education, Wellness." *American Libraries* vol. 37, issue 7 (2006): 7. https://search-ebscohost-com.ezp.lib.cwu.edu/login. aspx?direct=true&db=a9h&AN=21840757&site=ehost-live.

"Inaugural Banquet." *American Libraries* vol. 38, issue 7 (2007): 59. http://ezp.lib.cwu.edu/login?url=https://search.ebscohost.com/login.aspx?direct=true&db=a9h&AN=26279833&site=ehost-live.

"Indian Relocation Act of 1956." Wikipedia, The Free Encyclopedia, https://en.wikipedia.org/w/index.php?title=Indian_Relocation_Act_of_1956&oldid=947318878

"Loriene Roy." *American Libraries,* vol. 37, issue 3 (2006): 65. https://search-ebscohost-com.ezp.lib.cwu.edu/login.aspx?direct=true&db=a9h&AN=20033627&site=ehost-live.

Oder, Norman. "Roy Wins ALA Presidency." *Library Journal* vol. 131, issue 10 (2006): 16–16.

"Q&A: Loriene Roy, Outgoing ALA President," interview by Amelia Abreu, LibGig Archived 2010-04-25 at the Wayback Machine, March 19, 2010, audio.

"Q&A: Loriene Roy," interview by Patricia Cutright, February 24, 2020, audio.

Roy, Loriene. "Circle of Literacy." *American Libraries* vol. 38, issue 11 (2007): 6. http://ezp.lib.cwu.edu/login?url=https://search. ebscohost.com/login.aspx?direct=true&db=a9h&AN=27870794& site=ehost-live.

Roy, Loriene. "Leading a Fulfilled Life as an Indigenous Academic." *AlterNative: An International Journal of Indigenous Peoples* vol. 10, issue 3 (2014): 303–310. doi:10.1177/117718011401000308.

Staff. "Recognizing Gifts." *Library Journal* 130, March (2005): 41. http://ezp.lib.cwu.edu/login?url=https://search.ebscohost.com/login.aspx?direct=true&db=a9h&AN=16473341&site=ehost-live

Chapter 6

Bradley-Lopez, Gary. "UMKC Alumnus Sharice Davids Is Not Your Average Candidate." October 17, 2018. Retrieved April 26, 2020. https://info.umkc.edu/unews/umkc-alumnus-sharice-davids-is-not-your-average-candidate.

Brewer, Suzette. "Sharice Davids and the Rise of the Native Electorate." *Tribal College Journal* vol. 31, issue 2 (2019): 44–45. http://ezp.lib.cwu.edu/login?url=https://search.ebscohost.com/login.aspx?direct=true&db=a9h&AN=139658816&site=ehost-live.

Laviola, Erin. "Sharice Davids: 5 Fast Facts You Need to Know." Heavy.com. October 29, 2018. https://heavy.com/news/2018/10/sharice-davids.

Lowry, Bryan; Bergen, Katy. "Sharice Davids Makes History: Kansas' First Gay Rep, First Native American Woman in Congress." *Kansas City Star* (Kansas City), November 6, 2018.

Lowry, Bryan. "Not a Showoff. Sharice Davids' Quiet Approach Endears Her to Democratic Leaders." *Kansas City Star* (Kansas City), April 15, 2019. https://www.kansascity.com/article229177954.html

Raimondi, Marc. "From the Cage to Congress? Former MMA Fighter Sharice Davids Now Entering the Political Arena." *MMA Fighting.* March 14, 2018. https://www.mmafighting.com/2018/3/14/17038716/from-the-cage-to-congress-former-mma-fighter-sharice-davids-now-entering-the-political-arena

Stanley-Becker, Isaac. "Sharice Davids, Who Sees Past Discrimination As Her Asset, Could Become the First Gay Native American in Congress." *Washington Post* (Ithaca, New York), August 14, 2018.

Zidan, Karim. "How Sharice Davids Traded in MMA for a Shot at Political History." *The Guardian*, August 6, 2018.

"Frederick J. Davids, Obituary." The Amos Family Funeral Home. Retrieved April 26, 2020. https://www.amosfamily.com/frederick-j-davids.

"Sharice Davids' 10 Wins Historic Election in Congressional Race in Kansas." *Washington Post* (Ithaca, New York), November 8, 2018. Retrieved on April 26, 2020. https://www.washington post.com/news/morning-mix/wp/2018/08/14/sharice-davids-who-sees-past-discrimination-as-her-asset-could-become-the-first-gay-native-american-in-congress.

Chapter 7

Allison, Trish. "Roberta Jamieson Blazing a Trail." APTN National News, March 9, 2012. https://www.aptnnews.ca/author/admin/

Ball, Heather. *Great Women Leaders.* Toronto: Second Story Press, 2004.

Barnsley, Paul. 2004. "Jamieson Won't Run for Second Term." *Windspeaker* vol. 22. issue 8: 10. http://ezp.lib.cwu.edu/login?url=https://search.ebscohost.com/login.aspx?direct=true&db=a9h&AN=15081927&site=ehost-live.

Conn, Heather. "Roberta Jamieson." *The Canadian Encyclopedia,* July 17, 2019. https://thecanadianencyclopedia.ca/en/article/roberta-jamieson.

Lamberton, Dominique. "Ms. Chatelaine: Indigenous Advocate Roberta L. Jamieson." *Chatelaine,* June 1, 2016. https://www.chatelaine.com/living/ms-chatelaine-indigenous-advocate-roberta-l-jamieson.

McDermott, Julianna. "Roberta Jamieson, First Nations Activist, Shares Her Story on Makers." *Huffington Post Canada,* November 16, 2015.

National Speakers Bureau. "Roberta Jamieson." Retrieved April 2, 2020. https://www.nsb.com/speakers/roberta-jamieson.

New Federation House. n.d. "Roberta Jamieson, Mohawk, 1953, Native Leaders of Canada." Retrieved April 10, 2020. http://www.newfederation.org/Native_Leaders/Bios/Jamieson.htm.

Roberta Jamieson. 2019. "BCIT Honorary Doctorate of Technology." British Columbia Institute of Technology. October 23, 2018. Retrieved May 18, 2020. https://www.youtube.com/watch?v=lqvsYvYS2wo.

"Roberta Jamieson Bio." Canadian Council for Aboriginal Business. Retrieved April 16, 2020. https://www.ccab.com/events/past-events/2016-toronto-hot-topic-series/roberta-jamieson-bio.

"Roberta Jamieson to Say Farewell to Indspire." *Anishinabek News,* March 30, 2020. https://anishinabeknews.ca/2020/03/30/roberta-jamieson-to-say-farewell-to-indspire.

Chapter 8

Bendery, Jennifer. "At Last, We May Get Our First Native American Woman in Congress." HuffPost, February 22, 2018. https://www.huffpost.com/entry/deb-haaland-congress-native-american-woman_n_5a8c4249e4b00e986140253a.

Brave Noise Cat, Julian. "The First Native American Congresswoman in US History Could Be Elected This Year." *The Nation*, May 10, 2018. https://www.thenation.com/article/archive/the-first-native-american-congresswoman-in-us-history-could-be-elected-this-year.

"Congresswoman Deb Haaland." About, US House of Representatives. Retrieved May 4, 2020. https://haaland.house.gov/about.

Haaland, J.D. "Dutch." Obituary. *Albuquerque Journal*. Retrieved May 1, 2020. http://obits.abqjournal.com/obits/show/151921.

Haaland, Deb. "Haaland's Bill to Bolster Efforts to Address Missing and Murdered Indigenous Women's Crisis Clears House Natural Resources Committee." Vote Smart, Facts Matter. December 5, 2019. https://votesmart.org/public-statement/1389846/haalands-bill-to-bolster-efforts-to-address-missing-and-murdered-indigenous-womens-crisis-clears-house-natural-resources-committee#.XvJ6Y_J7luU.

Killough, Ashley. "Deb Haaland Redefines Congress: 'She'll Help Us See What Native Americans Mean." January 25, 2019. https://www.cnn.com/2019/01/25/politics/deb-haaland-profile-barrier-breakers/index.html.

Mehreen, Kasana. "Video of Deb Haaland Presiding over the House Is a Profound Moment in History." *The Hill*, March 7, 2019. http://hill.cm/hAidnd8.

Mettler, Lyn. "Rep. Debra Haaland Wears Traditional Native American Dress to Swearing-In Ceremony." *Today*, January 4, 2019. https://www.today.com/style/rep-debra-haaland-wears-traditional-native-american-dress-swearing-t146280.

Militare, Jessica. "Deb Haaland Is One of the First Native American Congresswomen—It Took Only Two Centuries." *Glamour*, November 9, 2018. https://www.glamour.com/contributor/jessica-militare.

Nelson, Rebecca. 2018. "Congress Has Never Heard a Voice Like Mine." *Newsweek Global* vol. 171, issue 20: 26–35.

Rickert, Levi. "Two American Indian Women Shatter the Glass Ceiling into Congress; Will Be Sworn In Today." *Native News Online*, January 3, 2019. https://nativenewsonline.net/currents/two-american-indian-women-shatter-the-glass-ceiling-into-congress-will-be-sworn-today.

Chapter 9

Burnett, Kristin, and Read, Geoff. 2012. *Aboriginal History: A Reader.* Don Mills, Ontario: Oxford University Press.

"Canada's First Woman Chief." *Indian Life* vol. 17 issue 1: 12, 1996. http://ezp.lib.cwu.edu/login?url=https://search.ebscohost.com/login.aspx?direct=true&db=a9h&AN=960560748&site=ehost-live.

"Elsie Knott." Directed by Sarah DeCarlo, Girls Action Foundation, produced by Final Fire Production. February 5, 2013. Audio 11:06. https://www.youtube.com/watch?v=N3giLrZIbCo.

"Elsie Knott." *Merle's Kaleidoscope of Life*, October 26, 2015. http://merles-kaleidoscope-of-life.blogspot.com.

Petten, Cheryl. 2006. "First Woman Chief Used Creativity to Solve Problems." *Windspeaker* vol. 23 issue 12: 26. http://ezp.lib.cwu.edu/login?url=https://search.ebscohost.com/login.aspx?direct=true&db=a9h&AN=1986138&site=ehost-live.

Skelly, Julia. "Elsie Knott." *The Canadian Encyclopedia.* Historica Canada. Article published October 17, 2018; last edited October 17, 2018. https://www.thecanadianencyclopedia.ca/en/article/elsie-knott.

Voyageur, Cora Jane. *Firekeepers of the Twenty-First Century First Nations Women Chiefs.* McGill-Queen's Native and Northern Series; 51. Montreal Quebec: McGill-Queen's University Press, 2008.

Wikipedia contributors, "Elsie Knott," Wikipedia, The Free Encyclopedia, Retrieved January 14, 2021. https://en.wikipedia.org/w/index.php?title=Elsie_Knott&oldid= 860654500.

Williamson, Kerry. "Female Chiefs Born to Lead: Bloodlines the Key in Dramatic Rise to Power of First Nations Women." *Calgary Herald* (Alberta, Canada). January 23, 2003. Thursday Final Edition. https://advance-lexis.com.ezp.lib.cwu.edu/api/document?collection=news&id=urn:contentItem:47RX-G720-01D6-M0CB-00000-00&context=1516831.

Chapter 10

Briggs, Kara. "Mary G. Ross Blazed a Trail in the Sky as a Woman Engineer in the Space Race, Celebrated Museum." *The National Museum of the American Indian*, October 7, 2009. https://blog.nmai.si.edu/main/2009/10/mary-g-ross-blazed-a-trail-in-the-sky-as-a-woman-engineer-in-the-space-race-celebrated-museum-.html.

Cherokee Heritage Center. Genealogy Links, Cherokee National Historical Society. 2010. http://www.cherokeeheritage.org/cherokeeheritagegenealogy-html/seminary-records.

Cook, Roy. "Cherokee Stories and Mary G. Ross Who Blazed a Path in the Space Race." http://www.americanindiansource.com/ross%20story/ross.html. Retrieved August 9, 2018.

Meredith, Howard. "Ross, Mary G." *American Indian Biographies,* rev. ed., edited by Carole A. Barrett, et al., Salem Press, 2005, pp. 437–438. https://link-gale-com.ezp.lib.cwu.edu/apps/doc/CX3035700308/GVRL?u=cwu_main&sid=GVRL&xid=e51a8784.

"Remembering Mary G. Ross—First American Indian Woman Engineer." *All Together.* Society of Women Engineers, August 9, 2018. https://alltogether.swe.org/2018/08/remembering-mary-g-ross-first-american-indian-woman-engineer.

Sheppard, Laurel M. Portfolio: Profile & Biographies: An Interview with Mary Ross, Lash Publications Intl. 1999. Retrieved January 14, 2021. Retrieved from http://www.nn.net/lash/maryross.htm.

"Video: Mary G. Ross—First American Indian Woman Engineer—Appears on 'What's My Line?'" *Society of Women Engineers Magazine.* Spring 2018. Retrieved August 9, 2018. Video of program included in article.

Viola, Herman. "Mary Golda Ross: She Reached for the Stars." *NMAI Magazine.* Winter 2018, pp. 16–21.

"Mary G. Ross" Wikipedia, The Free Encyclopedia. https://en.wikipedia.org/wiki/Mary_G._Ross Retrieved December 8, 2019.

Williams, Jasmin K. "Mary Golda Ross: The First Native American Female Engineer." *Amsterdam News.* New York. Archived from the original on April 10, 2013.

Weimers, Leigh. "The Sky was the Limit for this Teacher from Cherokee County." *San Jose Mercury News* (California). October 30, 1994.

Chapter 11

Heather Dawn Thompson. 2016. "Heather Dawn Thompson Enabling Investment Opportunities in Indian Country." SOCAP18 conference, YouTube video, 17:09. https://www.youtube.com/watch?v=UZOOq3QgDkw.

Bull, Bryan. "Native American Voters Drawing More Attention." *NPR Weekend,* "All Things Considered." October 30, 2004. https://advance-lexis-com.ezp.lib.cwu.edu/api/document?collection=news&id=urn:contentItem:4DNX-W0P0-TWD3-72RG-00000-00&context=1516831.

Horwitz, Sari. "A Man of Healing, a Saga of Suffering." *Washington Post.* December 29, 2014. https://advance-lexis-com.ezp.lib.

cwu.edu/api/document?collection=news&id=urn:contentItem: 5DY7-KJ61-JBFW-C00M-00000-00&context=1516831

Horwitz, Sari. "Dakota Boys' Left Mark on Tribal Justice." *Washington Post.* February 19, 2015. https://advancelexis-com. ezp.lib.cwu.edu/api/document?collection=news&id=urn:contentI tem:5FBH-9GF1-DYX1-H2HN-00000-00&context=1516831

Groves, Stephen. "As SD Gov. Opposes Hemp, Tribes See Opportunity." *The Bismarck Tribune.* December 2, 2019. https:// advance-lexis-com.ezp.lib.cwu.edu/api/document?collection= news&id=urn:contentItem:5XMY-2BW1-F039-F32P-00000-00 &context=1516831

Dupree, Suzanne. "Dupree-Dupris-Dupuis Family Tree for Looking Back Woman–Suzanne Dupree." *Looking Back Woman.* Retrieved April 22, 2020. https://lookingbackwoman.wordpress.com.

Targeted News Service. "Greenberg Traurig's Heather Dawn Thompson Speaks at 2019 SEC Government-Business Forum." Targeted News Service. August 27, 2019. https://advance-lexis-com.ezp. lib.cwu.edu/api/document?collection=news&id=urn:contentItem: 5WY8-KVW1-DYG2-R2C8-00000-00&context=1516831

Ziebach County Historical Society. *South Dakota's Ziebach County: History of the Prairie.* (Dupree, SD: State Publishing Co., 1982.)

Chapter 12

Ayer, Tammy. "Women Laud Effort to Curb Violence." *Yakima Herald-Republic* (WA), February 11, 2018: 1A. NewsBank: Access World News. https://infoweb-newsbank-com.ezp.lib.cwu.edu/apps/ news/document-view?p=AWNB&docref=news/16A286CD62B 6A860.

Banse, Tom. "A Yakama Woman's Promise to Her Elders Sheds Light on a Forgotten Northwest War." Northwest Public Radio, November 29, 2018. Audio, 7:45. https://www.nwpb.org/2018/11/29/ a-yakama-womans-promise-to-her-elders-sheds-light-on-a-for-gotten-northwest-war.

Bommerback, Jana. "Miss Yakama Nation's Yakama War: Emily Washines Brings Together Historic Enemies to Rewrite History." *Truewest: History of the American Frontier.* June 6, 2018. https:// truewestmagazine.com/miss-yakama-nations-yakama-war.

Yakima Herald-Republic Editorial Board. "Yakima Herald-Republic Coverage of Missing and Murdered Indigenous Women and Girls." *Yakima Herald-Republic,* March 13, 2020.

Huynh, Yen. "Interview with Emily Washines, MPA Tribal Governance Alumna." The Evergreen State College, February 19, 2019. https://www.evergreen.edu/mpa/post/interview-emily-washines-mpa-tribal-governance-alumna.

Jensen, Billy and Paul Holes. "Missing and Murdered Indigenous Women." *The Murder Squad,* September 30, 2019. Audio, 77:00. https://www.stitcher.com/podcast/exactly-right/jensen-and-holes-the-murder-squad/e/64251888.

Native Friends. n.d. "Emily Washines Biography." Accessed June 10, 2020. https://nativefriends.com/pages/about-me.

Rosane, Eric. "New BoT Member Brings a Yakima Native Perspective to the Table." *Observer*, Central Washington University, November 30, 2017.

Washines, Emily. "Who Are the Missing Native Women and How Do We Find Them?" Crosscut, Cascade Public Media, June 20, 2019, updated August 15, 2019. https://crosscut.com/2019/06/who-are-missing-native-women-and-how-do-we-find-them.

Washines, Emily. "Emily's Graduation Speech." The Evergreen State College, July 13, 2010. Audio 5:26. https://www.youtube.com/watch?v=nRNMmxPvJbE.

Washines, Emily and Gerald Peltier, "Natural Restoration and Cultural Knowledge of the Yakama Nation." Enduring Legacies Native Cases Initiative, The Evergreen State College. Retrieved January 14, 2021. http://nativecases.evergreen.edu/collection/cases/natural-restoration-yakama-nation.

Page 2: Courtesy of Oscar Pastenes

Page 5: Courtesy of Ashley Callingbull Burnham

Page 11: Courtesy of Montana State University

Pages 18, 20, 23: Courtesy of Office of Representative Ruth Anna Buffalo

Page 26: Courtesy of Pete Souza, White House

Pages 34, 36: Courtesy of Della Nohl

Pages 39, 40: Courtesy of Loriene Roy

Pages 43, 46, 49, 50: Courtesy of the Office of Congresswoman Sharice Davids

Page 53: Courtesy of Indspire

Page 56: Courtesy of Candice Ward/Indspire

Pages 60, 63, 66: Courtesy of the Office of Congresswoman Deb Haaland

Pages 69, 72, 75: Courtesy of Rita Rose

Pages 80, 83: Courtesy of Society of Women Engineers Records, Walter P. Reuther Library, Wayne State University

Page 86: Courtesy of the US Mint

Page 89: Courtesy of Nancy Musinguzi, Bush Foundation

Pages 91, 92: Courtesy of Heather Dawn Thompson

Page 95: Courtesy of Kenneth Girrard

Page 99: Courtesy of Central Washington University, photo by Photonuvo

Page 117: Courtesy of Kenneth Girrard

Patricia Cutright is Lakota and an enrolled member of the Cheyenne River Sioux tribe. Her love affair with books began at the age of six, when she convinced the city librarian that she was capable of reading her first Nancy Drew mystery, and then she blazed through all that was on the shelf in a matter of months. Her destiny was set while she worked at the university library as a student and her supervisor "informed" her that she would be a librarian. The rest is history, as they say. Patricia has lived in many places, from Brooklyn, New York, to the Federated States of Micronesia and many places in between, providing leadership in libraries along the way.

She has published articles and written book chapters on library technology and cooperation. Her awards include the 2003 American Library Association/LITA Gaylord Award for Achievement in Library and Information Technology, 2002 Oregon Librarian of the Year, 2017 University of Washington iSchool Distinguished Alumnus Award, and 2016 Presidential Administrator Award from Central Washington University. She has retired from library work but is busier than ever with travel, volunteering, and keeping the garden growing.

Patricia Cutright with her husband.

7th Generation publications celebrate the stories and achievements of Native people in North America through fiction and biography.

The **Native Trailblazer Series** for adolescent readers provides inspiring role models of Native men and women whose lives have had a positive impact in their communities and beyond.

For more information, visit:
nativevoicesbooks.com

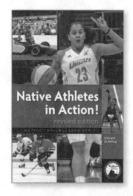

Native Men of Courage
REVISED EDITION
Vincent Schilling
978-1-939053-16-9 • $9.95

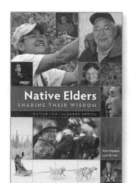

**Native Elders:
Sharing Their Wisdom**
Kim Sigafus and Lyle Ernst
978-0-9779183-6-2 • $9.95

**Native Writers:
Voices of Power**
Kim Sigafus and Lyle Ernst
978-0-9779183-8-6 • $9.95

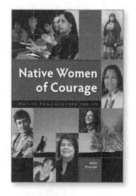

Native Athletes in Action!
REVISED EDITION
Vincent Schilling
978-1-939053-14-5 • $9.95

**Native Women
of Courage**
Kelly Fournel
978-0-9779183-2-4 • $9.95

**Native Musicians
in the Groove**
Vincent Schilling
978-0-9779183-4-8 • $9.95

Available from your local bookstore, or you can buy them directly from:
Book Publishing Company • PO Box 99 • Summertown, TN 38483 • 888-260-8458
Free shipping and handling on all orders.